A-Z WEYMOUTH &

CONTEN...

Ind...
Villa...
& selected Places of Interest

REFERENCE

A Road	A35	Car Park (Selected)	P
Proposed		Church or Chapel	†
		Cycleway (Selected)	
B Road	B3157	Fire Station	◼
Dual Carriageway		Hospital	Ⓗ
One-way Street		House Numbers (A & B Roads only)	298 77
Traffic flow on A Roads is also indicated by a heavy line on the driver's left.		Information Centre	𝒊
Restricted Access		National Grid Reference	³65
Pedestrianized Road		Park & Ride	Norden P+🚌
Track / Footpath		Police Station	▲
Residential Walkway		Post Office	★
Railway	Heritage Station / Station / Tunnel / Level Crossing	Toilet: without facilities for the Disabled	▽
		with facilities for the Disabled	▽
Built-up Area	WEST RD	Viewpoint	☀ ☀
		Educational Establishment	◢
Beach		Hospital or Hospice	◢
		Industrial Building	◢
Local Authority Boundary		Leisure or Recreational Facility	◢
Posttown Boundary		Place of Interest	◢
Postcode Boundary (within posttown)		Public Building	◢
		Shopping Centre or Market	◢
Map Continuation	12	Other Selected Buildings	◢

SCALE

1:15,840   4 inches to 1 mile   6.31 cm to 1 km   10.16 cm to 1 mile

0	¼	½	¾	1 Mile

0	250	500	750	1 Kilometre

Copyright of Geographers' A-Z Map Company Limited

Fairfield Road, Borough Green, Sevenoaks, Kent TN15 8PP
Telephone: 01732 781000 (Enquiries & Trade Sales)
                    01732 783422 (Retail Sales)

www.a-zmaps.co.uk

Copyright © Geographers' A-Z Map Co. Ltd.

Ordnance Survey® This product includes mapping data licensed from Ordnance Survey® with the permission of the Controller of Her Majesty's Stationery Office.

© Crown Copyright 2005. All rights reserved. Licence number 100017302

Edition 3* 2006

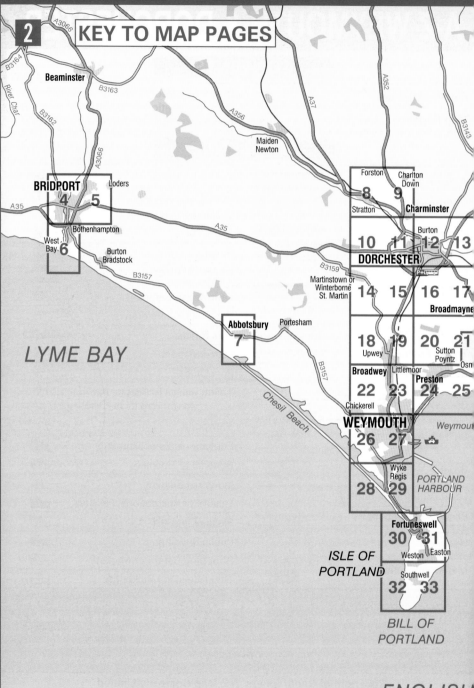

2 | KEY TO MAP PAGES

A3066

Beaminster

B3163

B3164

River Char

B3162

A356

Maiden Newton

A37

A352

B3143

BRIDPORT **4** **5** Loders

A35

Bothenhampton

A35

West Bay **6**

Burton Bradstock

B3157

Forston **8** **9** Charlton Down

Stratton

Charminster

Burton

10 **11** **12** **13**

DORCHESTER

B3159

Martinstown or Winterborne St. Martin **14** **15** **16** **17**

Broadmayne

LYME BAY

Abbotsbury **7** Portesham

Chesil Beach

B3157

18 **19** **20** **21**
Upwey Sutton Poyntz

Osn

Broadwey Littlemoor **Preston**
22 **23** **24** **25**

Chickerell

WEYMOUTH
26 **27**

Weymou

Wyke Regis
28 **29** *PORTLAND HARBOUR*

Fortuneswell
30 **31**

ISLE OF PORTLAND

Weston Easton

Southwell
32 **33**

BILL OF PORTLAND

ENGLISH

SCALE

0   1   2 Miles

0   1   2   3 Kilometres

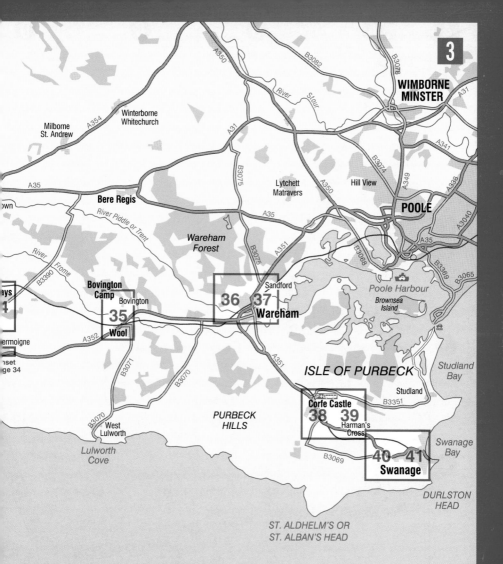

WIMBORNE MINSTER

A350
B3092
B3078
A31

River Stour

A354
Winterborne Whitechurch
A31
Hill View
POOLE

Milborne St. Andrew
A341

A35
Bere Regis
River Piddle or Trent
B3075
Lytchett Matravers
A350
A349
A338
A3040

own

A35
A35
A35
B3075
B3074

River Frome
Wareham Forest
A351
B3068
Poole Harbour
B3369
B3065

B3390
Sandford
36 37
Wareham
Brownsea Island

Bovington Camp
Bovington
35
Wool

ays
1

ermoigne

nset
ge 34

A352
B3071
B3070
A351

ISLE OF PURBECK
Studland Bay

Studland
B3351

West Lulworth
PURBECK HILLS
Corfe Castle
38 39
Harman's Cross

Swanage Bay

B3070
B3069
40 41
Swanage

Lulworth Cove

DURLSTON HEAD

ST. ALDHELM'S OR ST. ALBAN'S HEAD

CHANNEL

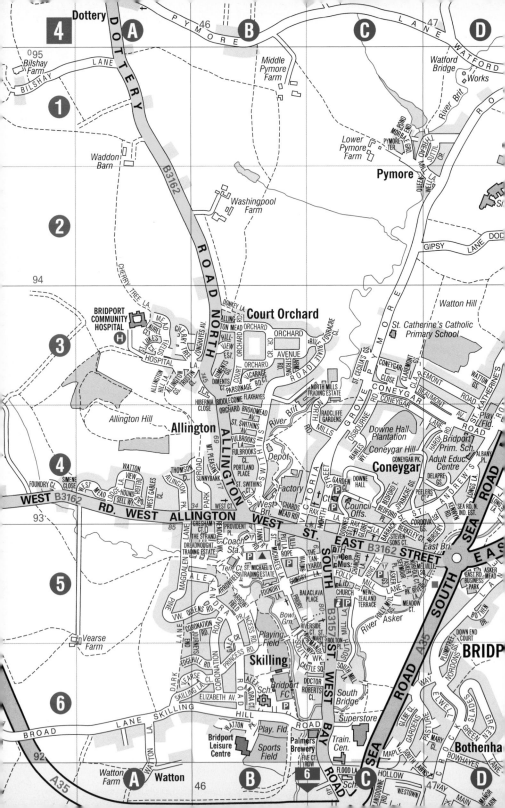

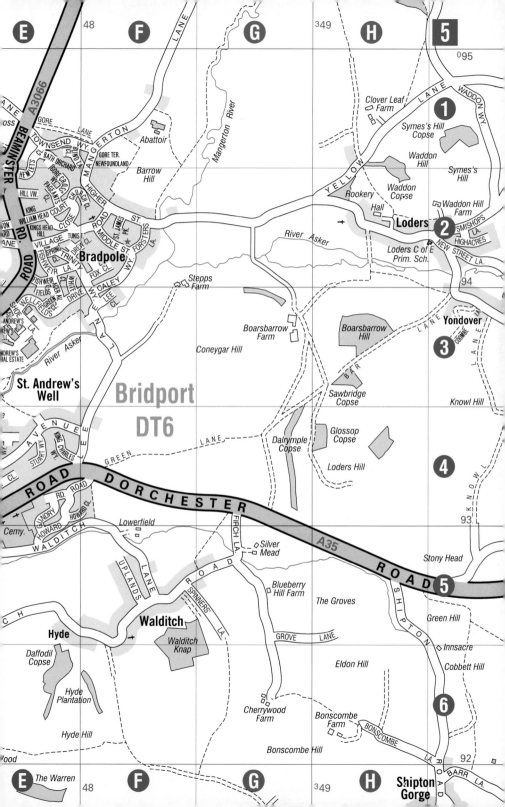

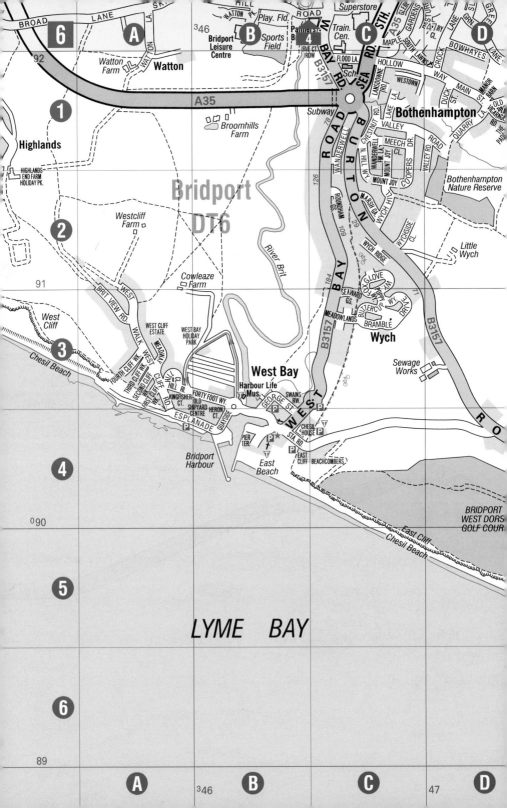

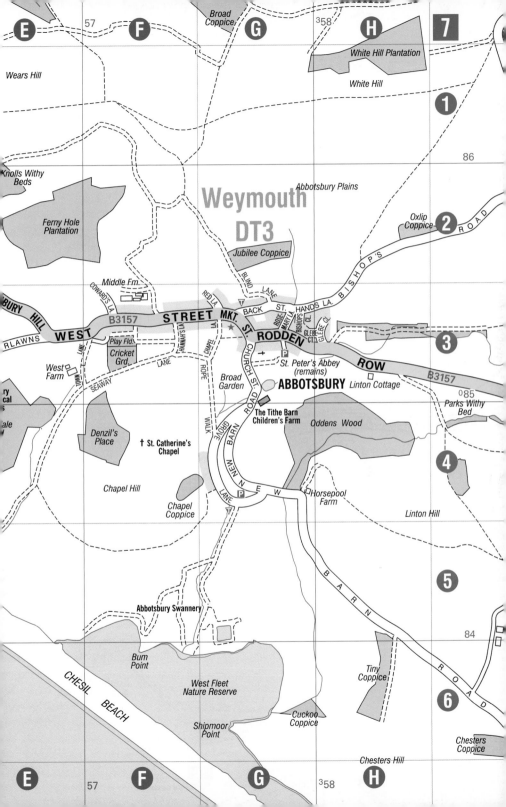

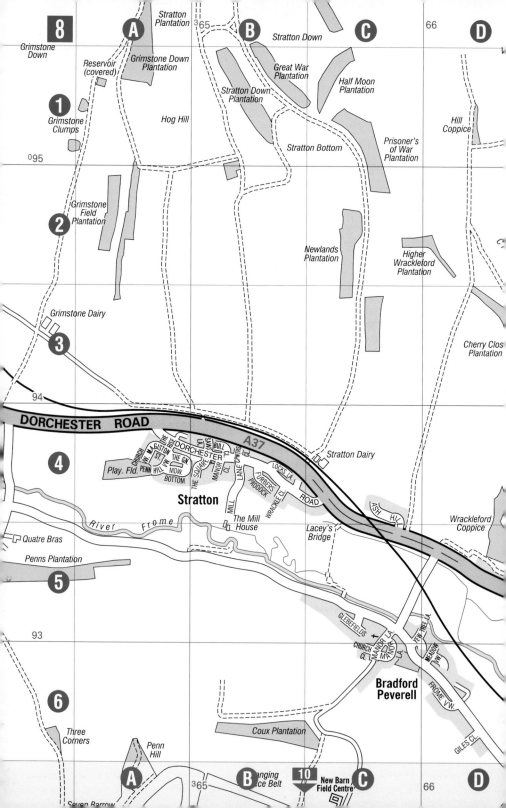

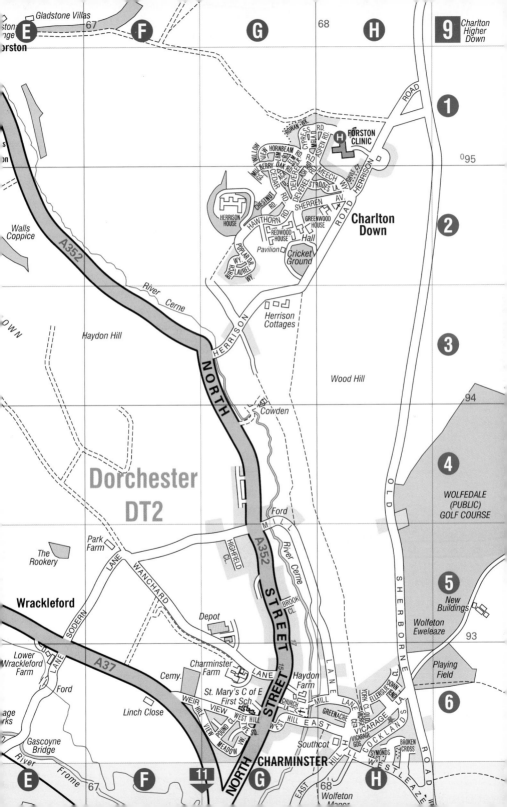

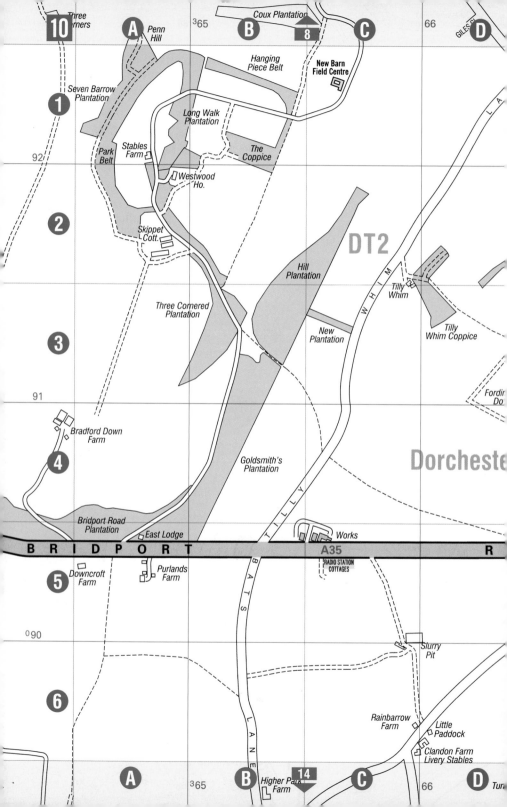

CHARMINSTER
Wolfeton
Wolfeton Manor
Wolfeton House
Westleaze House
Lower Burton Farm
Longwalls Coppice
Long Barrow
Long Coppice
River Frome
River Cerne
Whitfield Farm
Roman Aqueduct
Fordington Bottom
Square Coppice
Roman Aqueduct
DORCHESTER
RAILWAY TRIANGLE CARAVAN PARK
Cemetery
DT1
Poundbury
Works
DORSET COUNTY HOSPITAL
Damer's First Sch.
Children's Cen.
Nursery Sch.
Sports Pitches
Thomas Hardye Leis. Cen.
The Thomas Hardye Sch.
Club House
Rugby Football Ground
Playing Field
Play. Fld.
Ten. Cts.
Dorchester Mid. Sch.
The Prince of Wales Sch.
Playgrnd.
dington Field
A37
A352
B3147
B3150
B3144
A35
DORCHESTER BY-PASS
BRIDPORT ROAD
DAMER'S ROAD
NORTH ST.
WESTLEAZE
OLD SHERBORNE RD.
POUNDBURY RD.
CHESTNUT WAY
PEVERELL AVENUE
CAMBRIDGE RD.
COBURG RD.
QUEEN'S AVENUE
MAIDEN CASTLE ROAD
WEYMOUTH AVENUE
9
15
12
E F G H
1 2 3 4 5 6
67
68
71
90
91
92

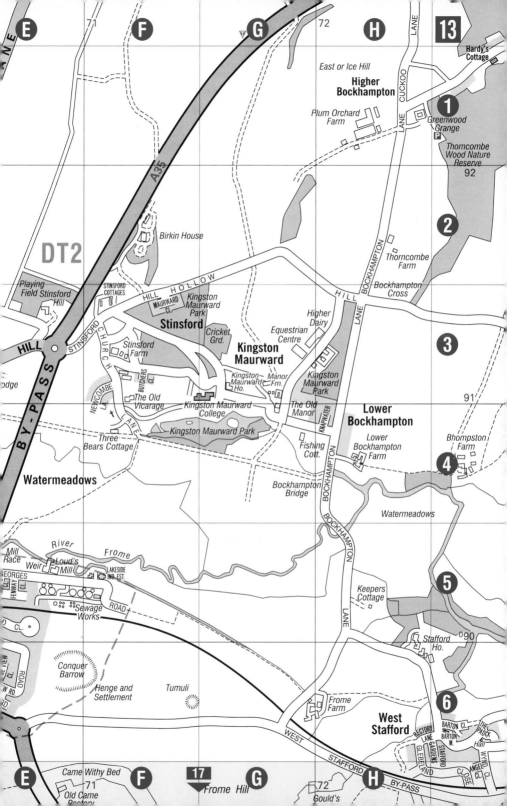

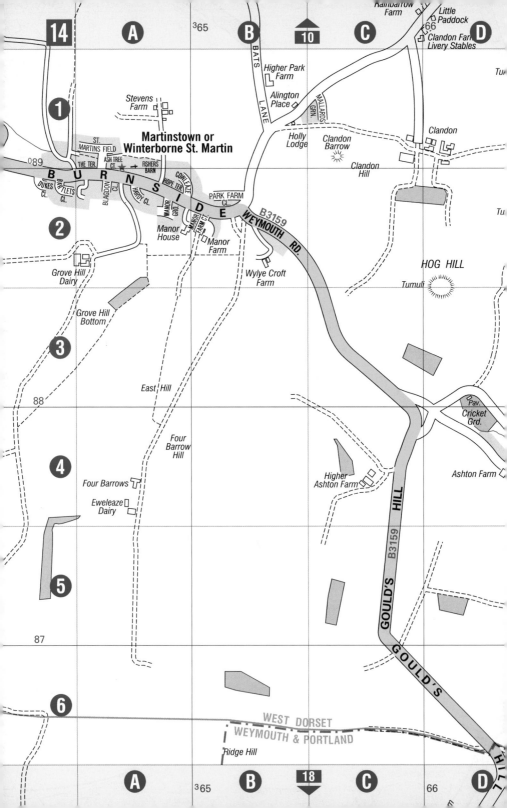

A   ³65   B   10   C   D

Rainbarrow Farm

Little Paddock

66

Clandon Farm Livery Stables

1

Stevens Farm

Higher Park Farm

Alington Place

GRN.

MALLARDS

Clandon

Martinstown or Winterborne St. Martin

ST. MARTINS FIELD

THE TER.

ASH TREE CT.

FISHERS BARN

Holly Lodge

Clandon Barrow

Clandon Hill

⁰89

B U R N S I D E

DUKES CL.

BARTLETS CL.

BLAGDON CL.

HARDY CL.

HOPE TER.

COULEAZE

MANOR GRO.

PARK FARM CL.

B3159

WEYMOUTH RD.

2

Manor House

MANOR FARM CT.

Manor Farm

Wylye Croft Farm

HOG HILL

Grove Hill Dairy

Tumuli

Grove Hill Bottom

3

East Hill

88

Pav.

Cricket Grd.

4

Four Barrow Hill

Four Barrows

Higher Ashton Farm

Ashton Farm

Eweleaze Dairy

GOULD'S HILL

B3159

5

87

GOULD'S

6

WEST DORSET

WEYMOUTH & PORTLAND

HILL

Ridge Hill

A   ³65   B   18   C   66   D

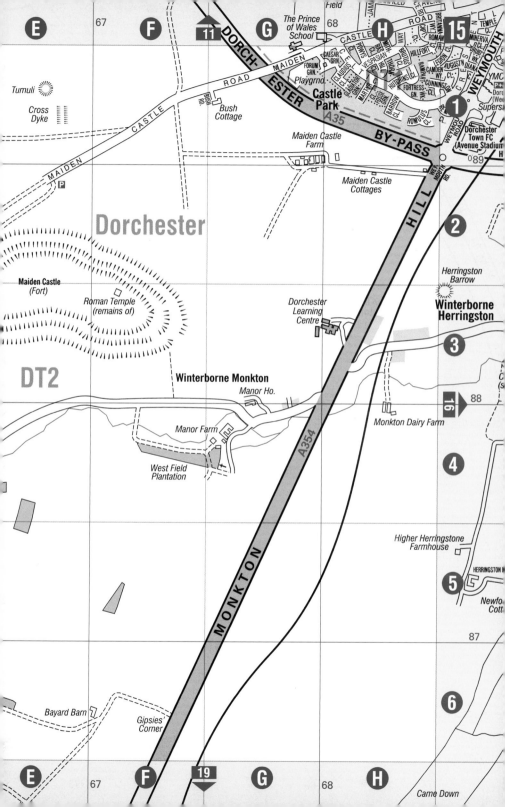

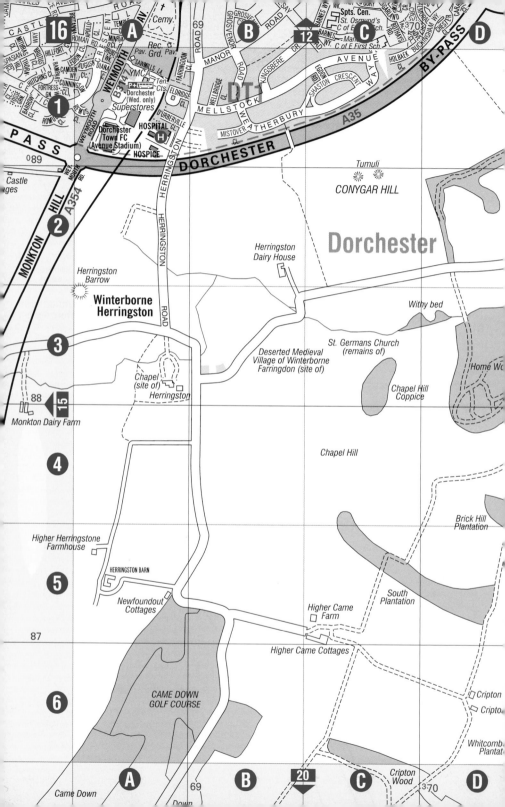

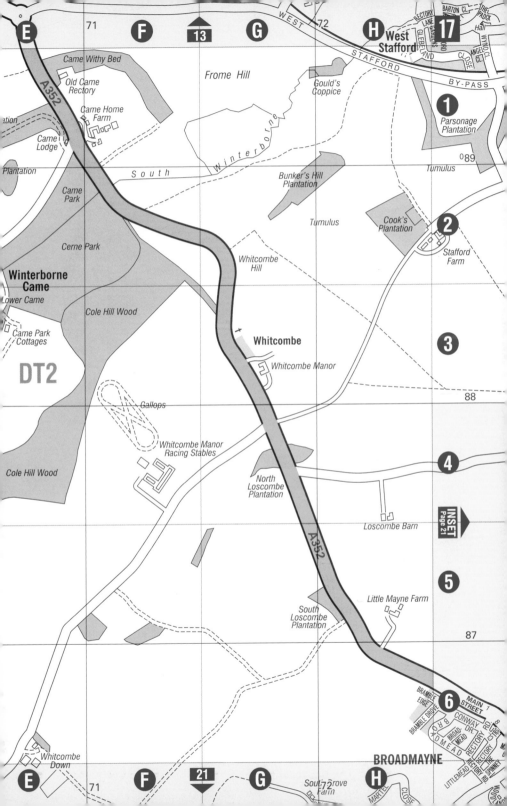

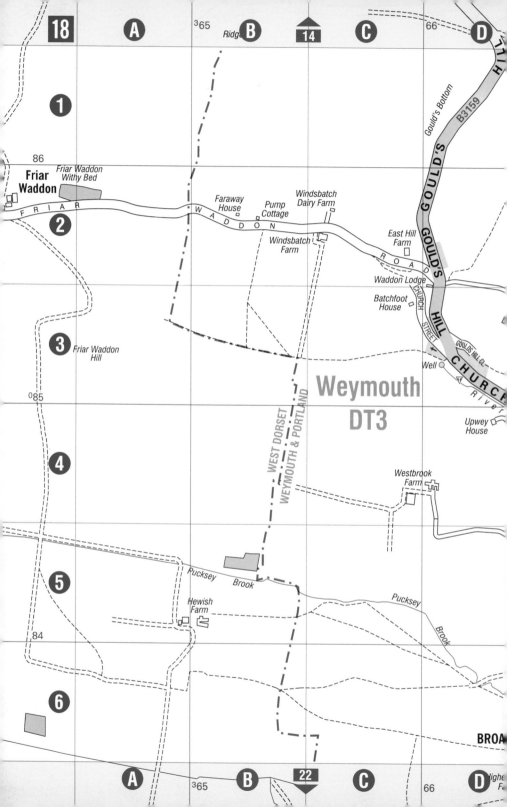

18

A   ³65   Ridg **B**   ▲14   **C**   66   **D**

1

86

Friar Waddon

Friar Waddon Withy Bed

F R I A R   W A D D O N

2

Faraway House   Pump Cottage   Windsbatch Dairy Farm

Windsbatch Farm

R O A D

East Hill Farm

Waddon Lodge

Batchfoot House

CHURCH STREET

GOULD'S HILL

GOULD'S HILL CL

Gould's Bottom

B3159

GOULD'S HILL

CHURCH

River

Well

3   Friar Waddon Hill

⁰85

Weymouth DT3

Upwey House

4

Westbrook Farm

WEST DORSET

WEYMOUTH & PORTLAND

5

Pucksey Brook

Pucksey Brook

Hewish Farm

84

6

A   ³65   **B**   ▽22   **C**   66   **D**

BROA

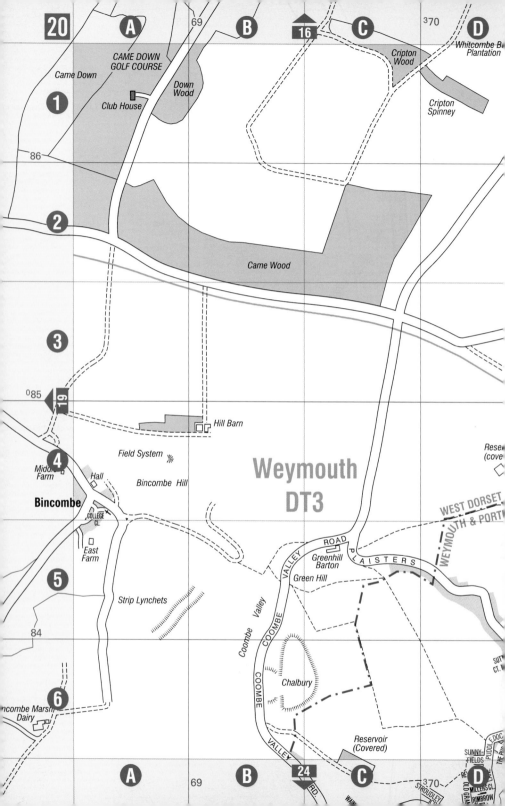

20
Ⓐ 69 Ⓑ ↑16 Ⓒ 370 Ⓓ

1
Came Down
CAME DOWN GOLF COURSE
Down Wood
Club House
Cripton Wood
Whitcombe B Plantation
Cripton Spinney

86

2
Came Wood

3

085
19
Hill Barn
Rese (cove

4
Field System
Midd Farm
Hall
Bincombe Hill
Weymouth DT3

Bincombe
COLLEGE CL.
East Farm

5
Strip Lynchets
WEST DORSET
WEYMOUTH & PORT
Greenhill Barton
Green Hill
ROAD
VALLEY
PLAISTERS

84
Coombe Valley
COOMBE
COOMBE
Chalbury
SUT CT.

6
ncombe Marsh Dairy
VALLEY
Reservoir (Covered)
SUNNY FIELDS
MILLERS CL.
PUDDLE DOC
RE
OLD GRIM
STROUDLEY
RIMBROW
THE PU

Ⓐ 69 Ⓑ ↓24 Ⓒ 370 Ⓓ

E   71   F   17   G   72   H   21

BRAMBLA B ROOK WAY DR RECTORY RD

BROADMAYNE

Whitcombe Down

INSET

BRIAR

HEAD RECTORY RD RE

RECTORY RD

ROA D

MARTEL CLOSE DROVE

1

SOUTH DROVE

South Drove Farm

SOUTH DROVE

Dorchester DT2

OSMINGTON DROVE

°86

2

BROOMHILL DROVE

C H A L K Y

Holcombe Valley Holiday Cottages

INSET

88

GABRIEL COTTS.

West Knighton Farm

Common Plantation

3

HARDY'S RW.

STAFFORD CL.

GLEBE CL

LEWELL

West Knighton

OAK WOOD

LANE

LANE

Broadmayne First School

4

rthdown Barn

SPRING GS.

Dorchester DT2

OLD BRICKFLD

°87

Cold Park Wood

WATERGATES

East Hill

White Horse

MAIN

BROADMAYNE

KNIGHTON

Sewage Works

5

CONWAY DR

BROAD-MEAD

CHAPEL

CHMN PADDOCK

BAKERS

LANE

SOUTH VIEW

ROMILL

RECTORY RD

BROADMEAD

ST. MARTINS CL

RECTORY RD

SPINNEY

CROSSTREE CL

CROSS

STREET

Fryer Mayne Ho.

WHITE HORSE LA.

Sutton Poyntz

LITTLEMEAD

FIRE

COWLEAZE RD

BEECH CL

Hall Play. Fld.

DROVE

HIGH TREES

55

60

Sundown

A352

6

ROAD

C H A L K Y

DRIVE

ROAD

The Old Stables

Friarmayne Farm

Charlmont Lodge

River   J o r d a n

OSMINGTON

Endigey

86

Ten Acres

ROMAN HILL BUSINESS PARK

E   25   F   71   G   373   H   Conygar Ho.

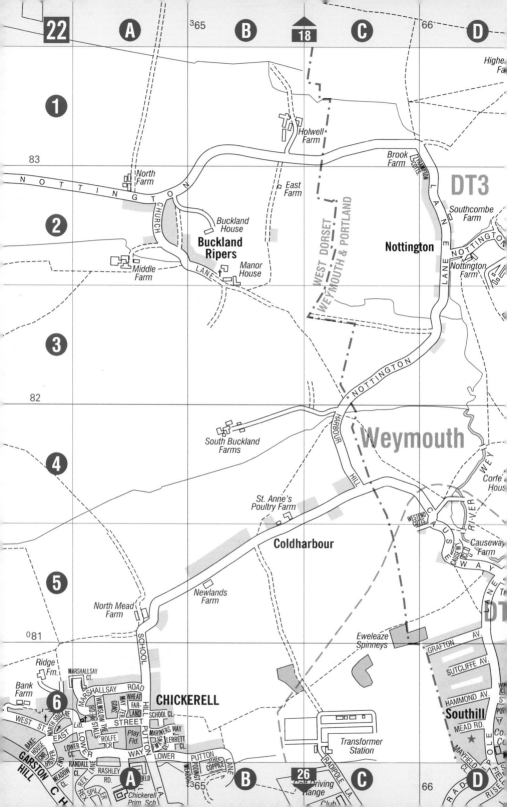

A ³65 B **18** C 66 D

1

Highe
Fa

Holwell
Farm

Brook
Farm

DT3

83
NOTTINGTON
North
Farm

East
Farm

Southcombe
Farm

2

Buckland
House

Nottington

Nottington
Farm

**Buckland
Ripers**

Middle
Farm

LANE

Manor
House

WEST DORSET
WEYMOUTH & PORTLAND

3

NOTTINGTON

82

South Buckland
Farms

HARBOUR

Weymouth

WEY

4

St. Anne's
Poultry Farm

HILL

Corfe
Hous

WESTEND
COTTS

Coldharbour

RIVER

Causeway
Farm

CAUSEWAY

5

Newlands
Farm

North Mead
Farm

Eweleaze
Spinneys

GRAFTON AV.

SUTCLIFFE AV.

D

081

Ridge
Fm.

MARSHALLSAY
CT.

MARSHALLSAY ROAD

HAMMOND AV.

Bank
Farm

6

WHEAT
FAR-
LAND

CHICKERELL

SCHOOL CL.

Southill

MEAD RD.

WEST ST.

NORTH SQUARE

STREET

MARINERS WAY

Play
Fld.

LERRETT CL.

MAYFIELD
CL.

BAKE-
HOUSE

LOWER

ROLFE
CR.

PUTTON

SCHOOL
HILL

LANE

PUTTON

THE
COPPICE

LANE

Transformer
Station

RADIPOLE LA.

RISE

GARSTON
HILL

REX LANE

RASHLEY
RD.

LOWER

PUTTON
MEAD

³65

26
Driving
Range
Club

RADIP

Chickerell
Prim Sch

A B 66 C D

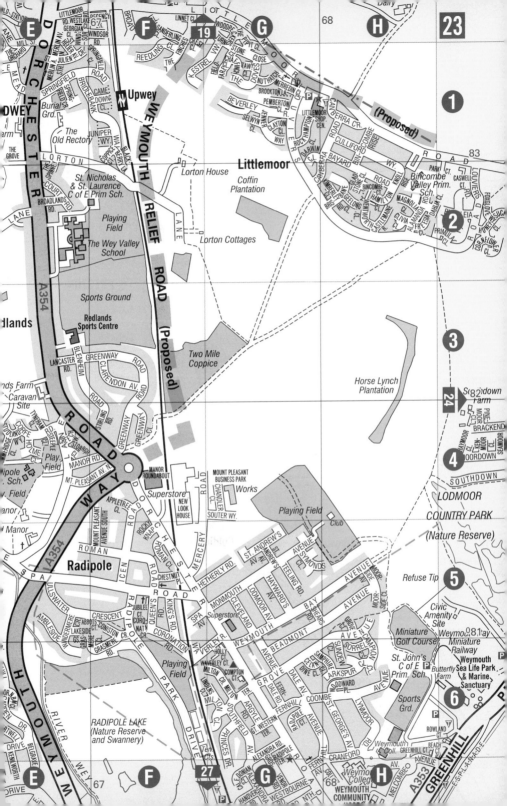

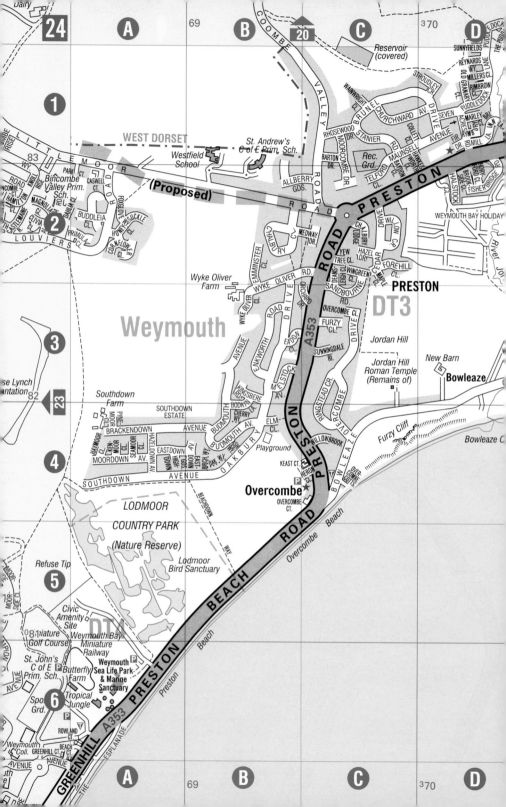

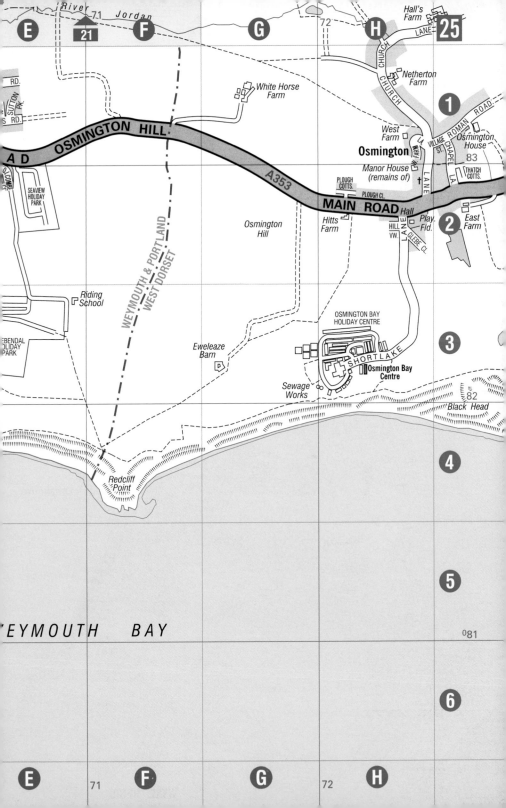

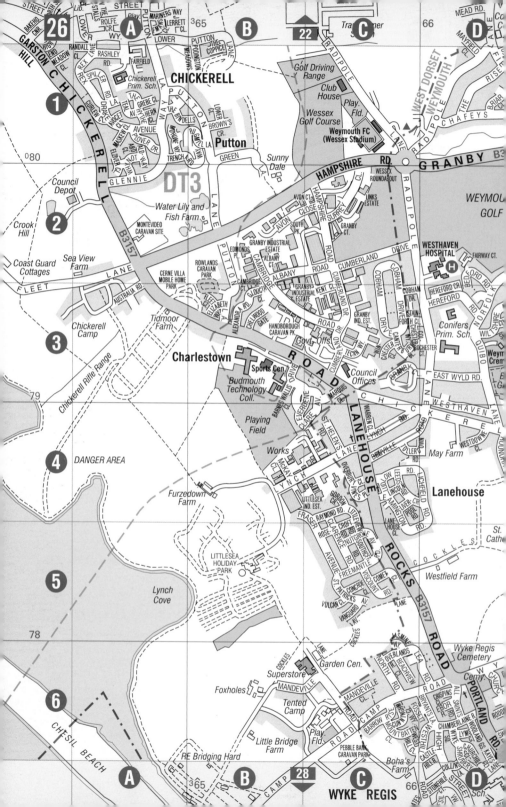

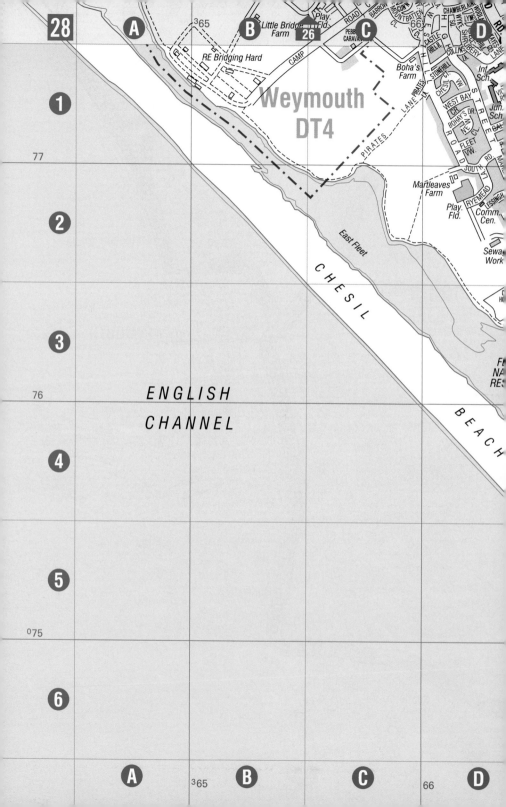

RYLAND'S

Playing Field

ST. DAVID'S

WYKE REGIS

ec. Grd.

SANDSFOOT HOLIDAY PK.

CASTLE COVE CARAVANS

◆ Sandsfoot Castle (Remains of)

Castle Cove

1

77

HILLCREST

DAWLISH CR.

DAWLISH CR.

HILL

BOURNE RD

DOWN

DOUGLAS

DUNDEE

DERWENT RD

■ Castle Cove Sailing Club

DOVER

Road

Road

Road

2

DUMBARTON

Bowl. Grn.

KINGFISHER

AVOCET CL.

SANDPIPER

PLOVER

FERRYBRIDGE

SCOTTS

SOWMAN

WHITEHEAD DR.

SMALLMOUTH CL.

OSPREY

Small Mouth

P O R T L A N D

3

PORTLAND

HARBOUR

76

esil Beach Centre

P

B E A C H

PORTLAND

4

5

075

A354

6

R O A D

Castletown Pier

DT5

Depot

OSPREY QUAY BUSINESS PARK

Portland Castle

BOSCAWEN CEN.

CASTLETOWN FLEET CT.

HMS Coastguard

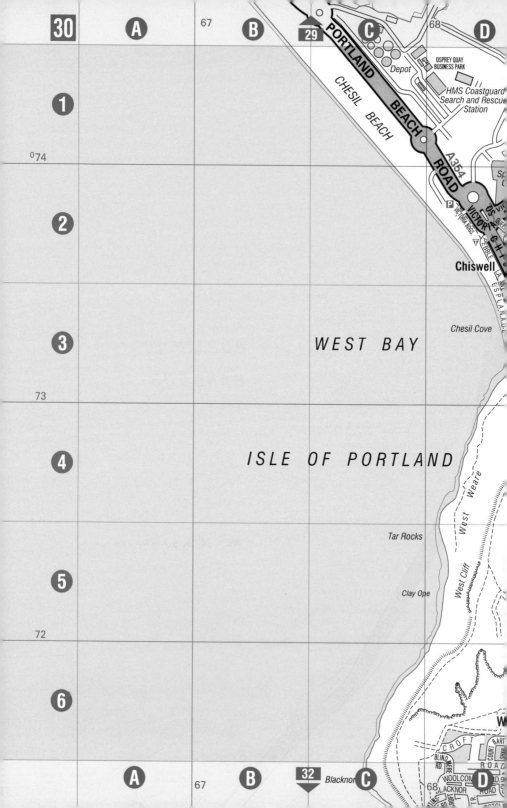

A 67 **B** 29 **C** 68 **D**

1

074

2

3

073

4

5

072

6

A 67 **B** 32 **C** 68 **D**

Depot

OSPREY QUAY
BUSINESS PARK

HMS Coastguard
Search and Rescue
Station

CHESIL BEACH

PORTLAND BEACH ROAD

A354

VICTORY

ESPLANADE

Chiswell

Chesil Cove

WEST BAY

ISLE OF PORTLAND

West Weare

Tar Rocks

West Cliff

Clay Ope

CROFT

BLIND
RD.

WOOLCOM

BLACKNOR

ROAD

Blacknor

1

71

2

3

ENGLISH
CHANNEL

070

4

5

69

6

Blacknor

Mutton Cove

WOOLCOMBE RD.
BLACKNOR
BLIND
MERE
RD.
CROFT
RD.
BAYCROFT RD.
MARINES
GRAVECROFT RD.
BOWERS
WESTCL
ROAD
WESTCL

WE

Gr

LINE

Southv
Prir
Sc

THE COURT-
YARD
CLIFF WAY
LEAP
REP
SANDS
SWEE
BARLANDS
CL
UN
164
SOUTH
SOUTHWELL
BUS. PK.
MARITIME
HOUSE
PORTLAND
SQ.
THE
SQUARE
WE
WAY
PORTLAND
HOUSE
COMPASS
TER.

Wallsend Cove

The Old Higher Lighthouse
Branscombe
Lodge

BILL

Lloyds Cottage

○ **Portland
Bird Observatory
& Field Centre**

Blow Hole

MOD
Site

PORTLAND

LIGHTHOUSE
VW.
Old
Coastguard
Cottages

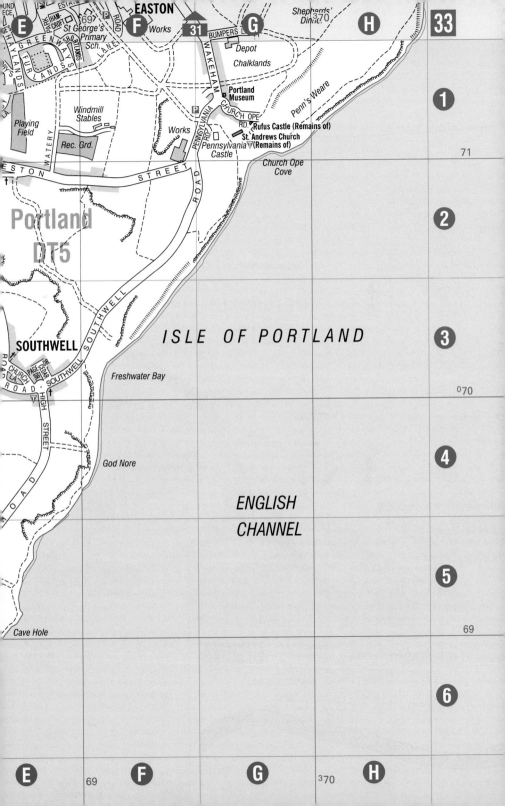

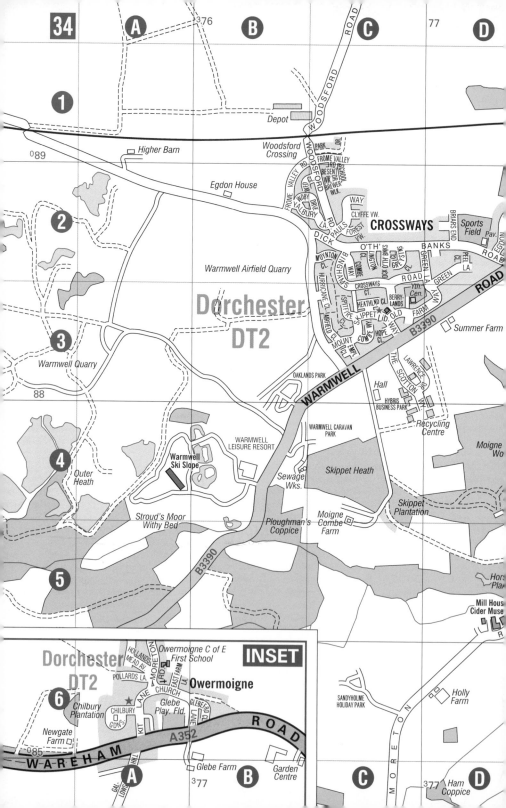

A 376 B ROAD C 77 D

1

Depot

0 89 Higher Barn Woodsford Crossing WOODSFORD ROAD PARK DR. FROME VALLEY

Egdon House FROME VALLEY RD. SCHOOL BESENT WK. BREWER WLK.

WOBY DRIVE WAY YALBURY LA. CLYFFE VW.

2 DICK PAULS LA. FOREST VW. **CROSSWAYS** BRIARS END EGDON ROAD Sports Field Pav.

Warmwell Airfield Quarry MOYNTON CL. BINGHAMS WAY HURRICANE CL. O'TH' COMMON LININGTON CL. COMBE WAY DICK O'TH' BNKS GREYSTNS CL. BANKS ROAD GREEN LA. GREEN WAY PEEL CL. LA.

3 SPITFIRE ST. ANFIELD CL. CROSSWAYS CT. HEATHLND CL. SKIPPET ST. COMPE WY. BERRY-LANDS FARM WAY OLD Ytth Cen. Lib. Summer Farm

Dorchester DT2

Warmwell Quarry MOUNT PL. HOPE CL. EMPL. WAY B3390

88 OAKLANDS PARK **WARMWELL** Hall LAWRENCE RD. THE SCOTTON

WARMWELL LEISURE RESORT Warmwell Ski Slope WARMWELL CARAVAN PARK HYBRIS BUSINESS PARK Recycling Centre Moigne Wo

4 Outer Heath Sewage Wks. Skippet Heath Skippet Plantation

Stroud's Moor Withy Bed B3390 Ploughman's Coppice Moigne Combe Farm

5 Hors Pla

Mill Hous Cider Muse

R

Dorchester DT2 HOLLANDS MEAD AV. Owermoigne C of E First School **INSET** SANDYHOLME HOLIDAY PARK Holly Farm

POLLARDS LA. MORETON RD. EAST FARM CHURCH **Owermoigne**

6 Chilbury Plantation CHILBURY GDN'S Glebe Play. Fld. GLEBELAND CLOSE GLEBELAND LANE

Newgate Farm KIT HILL CHURCH LANE **A352** **W A R E H A M R O A D**

0 85 GAL LONG HILL A Glebe Farm 377 B Garden Centre C MORETON 377 Ham Coppice D

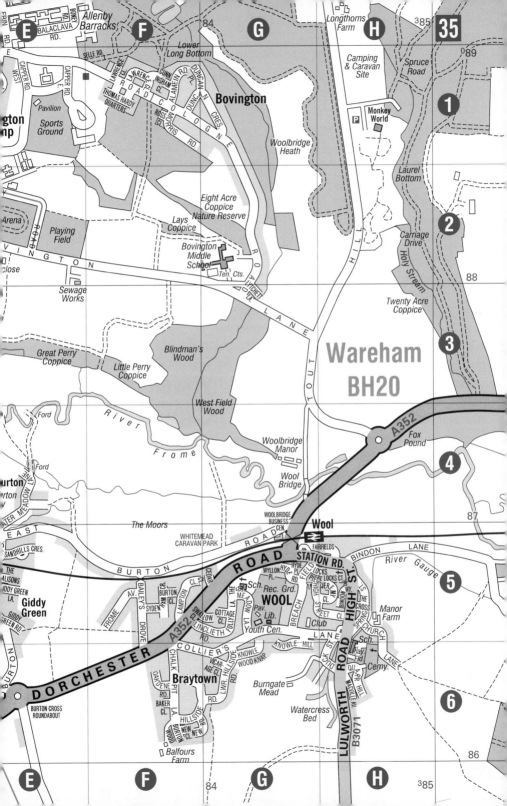

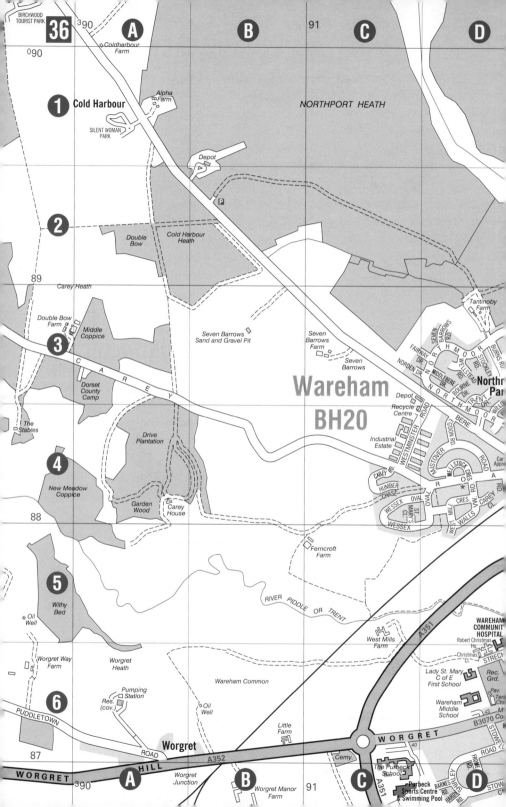

BIRCHWOOD TOURIST PARK

36

390 090

NORTHPORT HEATH

A **B** 91 **C** **D**

Coldharbour Farm

1 Cold Harbour

Alpha Farm

SILENT WOMAN PARK

Depot

2

Double Bow

Cold Harbour Heath

P

89

Carey Heath

Double Bow Farm

Middle Coppice

Seven Barrows Sand and Gravel Pit

Seven Barrows Farm

Tantinoby Farm

SEVEN BARROWS RD

FAIRWAY DR

WELLSTEAD DR

STOCKLEY RD

BURNS RD

3

C A R E Y

NORDEN DR

MIDDLEBERE DR

BOURNE DR

TRENT DR

NORTHMOOR DR

WILLO

Dorset County Camp

Seven Barrows

Wareham
BH20

Depot

North Pa

The Stables

Drive Plantation

Recycle Centre

WESTMINSTER

Industrial Estate

MINSTOVER

BERE RD

EDNOR RD

NORTHMOOR ROAD

Car Appro

4

New Meadow Coppice

Garden Wood

Carey House

CAREY RD

HUMBER CHASE

WESSEX

OVAL

ST. MARY'S CT.

CRES

WEST MILL RD

WELLSTOCK CRES

WEST WALLS

CAREY CL

R

O

A

88

WESSEX

OVAL

Ferncroft Farm

5

Withy Bed

Oil Well

RIVER PIDDLE OR TRENT

West Mills Farm

WAREHAM COMMUNIT HOSPITAL

A351

Robert Christmas Ho

Christmas Cl

STRECH

Worgret Way Farm

Worgret Heath

Wareham Common

Lady St. Mary C of E First School

Rec. Grd.

Pav. Ten Cts

6

PUDDLETOWN

Pumping Station

Res. (cov.)

Oil Well

Little Farm

Wareham Middle School

B3070 Co

STOWE

87

WORGRET

390

Worgret

ROAD

HILL

A352

A

Worgret Junction

B

Worgret Manor Farm

91

WORGRET

W O R G R E T

ROAD

ROME RD

HARLEY RD

C

A351

The Purbeck School

Purbeck Sports Centre & Swimming Pool

BARNES RD

D

Cemy.

40

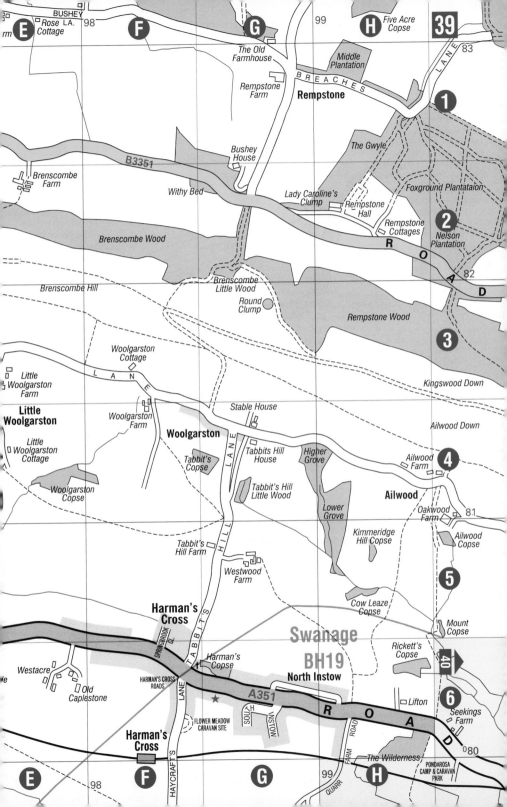

BUSHEY

E · Rose LA. Cottage · 98 · F · G · 99 · H · Five Acre Copse

The Old Farmhouse

Middle Plantation

Rempstone Farm

Rempstone

B R E A C H E S

1

The Gwyle

B3351

Brenscombe Farm

Bushey House

Lady Caroline's Clump

Foxground Plantataion

Withy Bed

Rempstone Hall

Rempstone Cottages

2

Nelson Plantation

R · O

Brenscombe Wood

82

A · D

Brenscombe Hill

Brenscombe Little Wood

Round Clump

Rempstone Wood

3

Woolgarston Cottage

L A N E

Kingswood Down

Little Woolgarston Farm

Woolgarston Farm

Stable House

Ailwood Down

Little Woolgarston

Woolgarston

Tabbits Hill House

Higher Grove

Ailwood Farm

4

Little Woolgarston Cottage

Tabbit's Copse

Tabbit's Hill Little Wood

Ailwood

Oakwood Farm · 81

Woolgarston Copse

H I L L

Lower Grove

Kimmeridge Hill Copse

Ailwood Copse

Tabbit's Hill Farm

Westwood Farm

5

Harman's Cross

Cow Leaze Copse

Mount Copse

Westacre

Old Caplestone

SPRINGBROOK

TABBITS

Harman's Copse

Swanage BH19

North Instow

Rickett's Copse

40

HARMAN'S CROSS ROADS

A351

S O U T H · I N S T O W

R · O · A

Lifton

6

Seekings Farm

Harman's Cross

FLOWER MEADOW CARAVAN SITE

FARM ROAD

The Wilderness

80

PONDAROSA CAMP & CARAVAN PARK

HAYCRAFT'S

E · 98 · F · G · 99 · QUARR · H

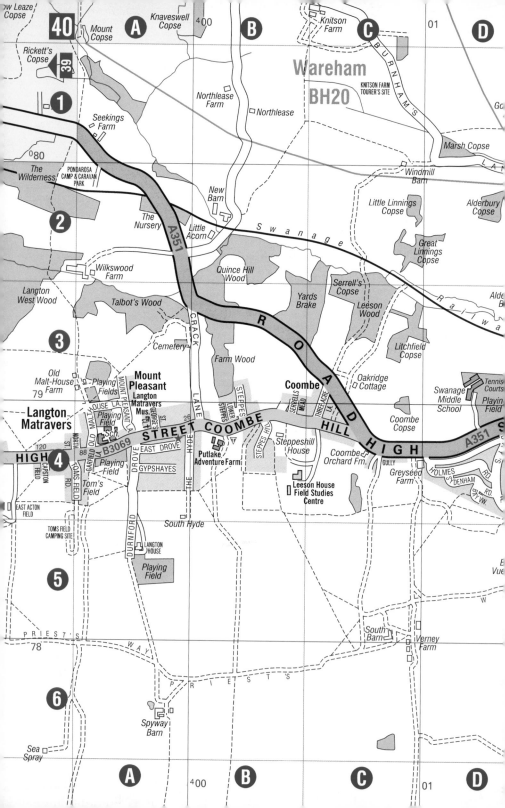

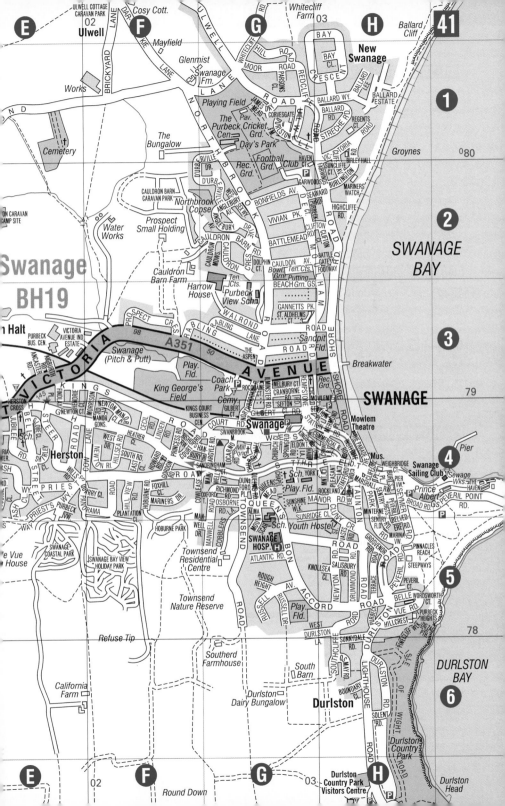

INDEX

Including Streets, Places & Areas, Hospitals & Hospices, Industrial Estates,
Selected Flats & Walkways, Stations and Selected Places of Interest.

HOW TO USE THIS INDEX

1. Each street name is followed by its Postcode District and then by its Locality abbreviation(s) and then by its map reference;
e.g. **Abbotsbury Rd.** DT4: Weym . . . .4E **27** is in the DT4 Postcode District and the Weymouth Locality and is to be found in square 4E on page **27**. The page number is shown in bold type.

2. A strict alphabetical order is followed in which Av., Rd., St., etc. (though abbreviated) are read in full and as part of the street name;
e.g. **Ashton Rd.** appears after **Ashley Rd.** but before **Ashton Rd.**

3. Streets and a selection of flats and walkways too small to be shown on the maps, appear in the index with the thoroughfare to which it is connected shown in brackets; e.g. **Acland Ct.** DT1: Dor . . . .5B **12** (off Linden Av.)

4. Addresses that are in more than one part are referred to as not continuous.

5. Places and areas are shown in the index in **BLUE TYPE** and the map reference is to the actual map square in which the town centre or area is located and not to the place name shown on the map; e.g. **BRIDPORT** 5C **4**

6. An example of a selected place of interest is Bridport Mus. 5C **4**

7. An example of a station is **Dorchester South Station (Rail)** . . . .5B **12**. Included are Rail **(Rail)** and Park & Ride **(Park & Ride)**

8. An example of a hospital or hospice is BRIDPORT COMMUNITY HOSPITAL 3A **4**

GENERAL ABBREVIATIONS

All. : Alley	**Cres.** : Crescent	**Ind.** : Industrial	**Rd.** : Road
App. : Approach	**Cft.** : Croft	**Info.** : Information	**Rdbt.** : Roundabout
Arc. : Arcade	**Dr.** : Drive	**La.** : Lane	**Shop.** : Shopping
Av. : Avenue	**E.** : East	**Lwr.** : Lower	**Sth.** : South
Bk. : Back	**Ent.** : Enterprise	**Mnr.** : Manor	**Sq.** : Square
Bri. : Bridge	**Est.** : Estate	**Mdw.** : Meadow	**Sta.** : Station
Bldgs. : Buildings	**Fld.** : Field	**Mdws.** : Meadows	**St.** : Street
Bus. : Business	**Flds.** : Fields	**M.** : Mews	**Ter.** : Terrace
Cvn. : Caravan	**Gdns.** : Gardens	**Mt.** : Mount	**Trad.** : Trading
C'way. : Causeway	**Gth.** : Garth	**Mus.** : Museum	**Up.** : Upper
Cen. : Centre	**Ga.** : Gate	**Nth.** : North	**Vw.** : View
Cl. : Close	**Gt.** : Great	**Pde.** : Parade	**Vs.** : Villas
Comn. : Common	**Grn.** : Green	**Pk.** : Park	**Vis.** : Visitors
Cnr. : Corner	**Gro.** : Grove	**Pas.** : Passage	**Wlk.** : Walk
Cotts. : Cottages	**Hgts.** : Heights	**Pl.** : Place	**W.** : West
Ct. : Court	**Ho.** : House	**Ri.** : Rise	**Yd.** : Yard

LOCALITY ABBREVIATIONS

A'bury : **Abbotsbury**	Cross : **Crossways**	Nott : **Nottington**	Upwey : **Upwey**
Binc : **Bincombe**	Dor : **Dorchester**	Osm : **Osmington**	Wald : **Walditch**
Both : **Bothenhampton**	Dot : **Dottery**	Over : **Overcombe**	Ware : **Wareham**
Bovin : **Bovington**	E'ton : **Easton**	Ower : **Owermoigne**	Warm : **Warmwell**
Brad P : **Bradford Peverell**	Fort : **Fortuneswell**	Pound : **Poundsbury**	Watt : **Watton**
Bradp : **Bradpole**	Friar W : **Friar Waddon**	Pres : **Preston**	W Bay : **West Bay**
Bridp : **Bridport**	Frome W : **Frome Whitfield**	Pym : **Pymore**	W Kni : **West Knighton**
Broadm : **Broadmayne**	Grim : **Grimstone**	Rad : **Radipole**	W Staf : **West Stafford**
Broadw : **Broadwey**	Har C : **Harman's Cross**	Red : **Redlands**	Westo : **Weston**
Buck R : **Buckland Ripers**	Higher B : **Higher Bockhampton**	Sand : **Sandford**	Weym : **Weymouth**
Burt : **Burton**	K'ton : **Kingston**	Ship G : **Shipton Gorge**	Win H : **Winterbourne Herringston**
Burt B : **Burton Bradstock**	K'ton M : **Kingston Maurward**	S'hill : **Southill**	Win M : **Winterbourne Monkton**
Cas : **Castletown**	Knit : **Knitson**	S'well : **Southwell**	W'ford : **Woodsford**
Charl D : **Charlton Down**	Lang M : **Langton Matravers**	Stin : **Stinsford**	Wool : **Wool**
Charm : **Charminster**	Lit : **Littlemoor**	Stob : **Stoborough**	Woolg : **Woolgarston**
Chick : **Chickerell**	Loders : **Loders**	Strat : **Stratton**	Wrac : **Wrackleford**
Cok F : **Coker's Frome**	Lwr B : **Lower Bockhampton**	Sut P : **Sutton Poyntz**	Wyke : **Wyke Regis**
Cold H : **Cold Harbour**	Lwr E : **Lower Eype**	Swan : **Swanage**	
Corfe C : **Corfe Castle**	Mart : **Martinstown**	U'ders : **Uploders**	

A

Aconbury Av. DT1: Pound 5F **11**
Adelaide Cres. DT4: Weym 3E **27**
Admirals Way BH20: Ware 3E **37**
Agra Pl. DT1: Dor 5B **12**
Aigburth Rd. BH19: Swan 3E **41**
AILWOOD 4H **39**
Airfield Cl. DT2: Cross 3C **34**
Alamanda Rd. DT3: Lit 2H **23**
Alamein Rd. DT3: Bovin 1F **35**
Albany Ct. DT1: Dor 5A **12**
    DT4: Weym 2B **26**
Albany Pl. DT6: Bridp 4D **4**
Albany Rd. DT4: Weym 2B **26**
Albert Rd. DT1: Dor 5A **12**
Albert St. DT4: Weym 3G **27**
Albert Ter. DT5: Fort 2D **30**

Acland Rd. DT1: Dor 4B **12**

ABBOTSBURY 3G **7**
Abbotsbury Hill. DT3: A'bury . . .3E **7**
Abbotsbury Rd. DT4: Weym . . .4E **27**
Abbotsbury Sub-Tropical Gdns.
    .3E **7**
Abbotsbury Swannery 5F **7**
Abbots Ct. DT3: Rad 5E **23**
Abbot's Quay BH20: Ware 6E **37**
Acacia Cl. DT4: S'hill 6E **23**
Acacia Dr. DT2: Charl D 2G **9**
Acer Av. DT6: Bradp 3E **5**
Ackerman Rd. DT1: Dor 5D **12**
Acland Ct. DT1: Dor 5B **12**
    (off Linden Av.)

Albert Vs. DT5: Fort 3D **30**
Albion Cres. DT5: Fort 2E **31**
Aldabrand Cl. DT3: Chick 1A **26**
Alder Cl. BH20: Sand 1H **37**
Alexandra Cl. DT6: Bridp 6B **4**
Alexandra Gdns.
    DT4: Weym 4H **27**
Alexandra Rd. DT1: Dor 5A **12**
    DT4: Weym 3B **26**
    DT4: Weym 6G **23**
                (Radipole)
    DT6: Bridp 5B **4**
Alexandra Ter. DT1: Dor 4B **12**
          (off Somerleigh Rd.)
Alfred Pl. DT1: Dor 5C **12**

Alfred Rd. DT1: Dor 5B
Alice Rd. DT1: Dor 5H
Alington Av. DT1: Dor 5D
Alington Rd. DT1: Dor 5C
Alington St. DT1: Dor 4B
Alington Ter. DT1: Dor 4B
Alisons, The BH20: Wool 5E
Allberry Gdns. DT3: Pres 2B
ALLINGTON 4B
Allington Gdns. DT6: Bridp 3A
Allington Hill La.
    DT6: Bridp 3A
Allington Mead DT6: Bridp 3B
Allington Pk. DT6: Bridp 4A
All Saints Rd. DT1: Dor 4C
    DT4: Wyke 6D
Alma Rd. DT4: Weym 3G

Alma Ter.—Buxton Cl.

Ter. BH19: Swan 4G 41
DT5: E'ton 5H 31
nd Gro. DT4: S'hill 6E 23
eside DT3: Rad 5E 23
ia Cl. DT5: Fort 2E 31
ns Rd. BH20: Bovin 1E 35
ster Rd. BH19: Swan 3E 41
l Cl. DT2: W Staf 1H 17
ebury Av. BH19: Swan ...2G 41
ebury Bus. Pk.
BH20: Ware 4E 37
ebury Ct. BH20: Ware 5E 37
ope Wlk. DT1: Dor 4B 12
Cl. BH19: Swan 4D 40
o Cl. DT1: Dor 6A 12
etree Cl. DT3: Rad 4F 23
on Cl. DT4: Weym 1F 29
tus Cl. DT1: Dor 5B 12
de Ter. *BH19: Swan......4H 41*
(off High St.)
e Rd. BH19: Swan 4G 41
DT4: Weym 6G 23
gton DT4: S'hill 1D 26
ada Way DT1: Dor 6D 12
strong Rd. DT6: Bridp 3B 4
em Grn. DT1: Dor 4H 11
wfield DT6: Bridp 5B 4
(not continuous)
t Row DT5: Fort 3E 31
Cl. BH19: Swan 4E 41
BH20: Sand 1G 37
Hill DT2: Strat 4C 8
ngton St. DT1: Pound 5G 11
ey Ct. DT4: Weym 4E 27
ey Rd. DT1: Dor 6B 12
Rd. DT2: Charl D 2G 9
on Rd. DT4: Weym 4F 27
Tree Ct. DT2: Mart 1A 14
Way DT3: Over 4B 24
r Gdns. DT6: Bridp 5C 4
r Mead DT6: Both 5D 4
r Ter. DT6: Bridp 5C 4
n, The BH19: Swan 3G 41
n Rd. DT2: Charl D 1H 9
d Way DT4: Weym 2H 27
lstan Rd. DT1: Dor 5C 12
ntic Rd. BH19: Swan 5G 41
usta Cl. DT5: E'ton 5G 31
ustan Cl. DT1: Dor 1A 16
usta Pl. *DT4: Weym 4H 27*
(off New St.)
usta Rd. DT5: E'ton 5G 31
ralia Rd. DT3: Chick 3A 26
anche Rd. DT5: S'well 2D 32
ue Rd. DT4: Weym 1H 27
nue Stadium 1A 16
et Cl. DT3: Chick 1A 26
DT4: Wyke 2E 29
Cl. DT4: Weym 2B 26
Ct. DT4: Weym 2B 26
Dr. BH20: Ware 4D 36
sley Ct. DT4: Weym 2F 27

B

eny Wlk. DT1: Pound 5F 11
Rivers La. DT6: Bridp 5C 4
k St. DT3: A'bury 3G 7
ey's Drove BH20: Wool 5F 35
ehouse Cnr. DT3: Chick ...6A 22
er Cl. BH20: Wool 6F 35
ers Paddock
DT2: Broadm 5H 21
clava Pl. DT6: Bridp 5B 4
clava Rd. BH20: Bovin ...1E 35
DT5: Cas 1G 31
ard Est. BH19: Swan 1H 41
ard Lee BH19: Swan 1H 41
ard Rd. BH19: Swan 1H 41
ard Way BH19: Swan 1H 41
moral Cres. DT1: Dor 6D 12
ton Shard DT6: Bradp 2E 5
clay Rd. DT4: Weym 4F 27
ake Ct. *DT1: Pound 5G 11*
(off Wardbrook St.)
ands Cl. DT5: S'well 3D 32
La. DT6: Loders 3H 5
eycroft Rd. DT5: Westo ...1D 32
Barley Way DT4: Weym 5H 27
Barnes Rd. BH20: Ware 6D 36
Barnes Wallis Cl.
DT3: Chick 4B 26
Barnes Way DT1: Dor 6C 12
(not continuous)
Barnhaven Cl. DT4: Weym 5E 27
Barrack Rd. DT4: Weym 4H 27
Barrack St. DT6: Bridp 5C 4
Barr La. DT6: Ship G 6H 5
Barrow Cl. DT1: Dor 1H 15
Barrow Ri. DT4: Wyke 6C 26
Bartlets Cl. DT2: Mart 2A 14
Barton Cl. DT2: W Staf 6H 13
Barton Dr. DT3: Pres 1C 24
Barton M. DT2: W Staf 6H 13
Bath Orchard DT6: Bradp 1E 5
Bathsheba Ter. *DT1: Dor 6C 12*
(off Lucetta La.)
Bath St. DT4: Weym 3G 27
Bats La. DT2: Dor, Mart 5B 10
Battle Gate Footway
BH19: Swan 2H 41
Battlemead BH19: Swan 2G 41
BH20: Corfe C 3B 38
Bayard Rd. DT3: Lit 1H 23
Baycliffe Rd. DT4: Weym 4E 27
Bay Cl. BH19: Swan 1H 41
Bay Cres. BH19: Swan 1H 41
Baydon Cl. DT3: Pres 2C 24
Bayeux Ct. DT1: Dor 5C 12
Baynard's Rd. DT1: Dor 5G 11
Bay Vw. BH19: Swan 4D 40
Beachcombers DT6: W Bay 4C 6
Beach Ct. DT4: Weym 6H 23
Beachdown Way DT3: Over ...4B 24
Beach Gdns. BH19: Swan 3G 41
Beachview Cl. DT4: Wyke 6C 26
Beaminster Rd. DT6: Bradp 1E 5
Beauchamp Ct.
BH19: Swan 3G 41
(off Victoria Av.)
Beaulieu DT4: S'hill 1E 27
Beaumont Av. DT4: Weym 6G 23
DT6: Bridp 3D 4
Bedford Pl. DT6: Bridp 4C 4
Bedford Rd. DT4: Weym 2D 26
Bedford Ter. DT6: Bridp 4C 4
Beech Cl. DT2: Broadm 6G 21
Beech Ct. DT1: Dor 5B 12
Beeches, The BH20: Sand 1G 37
Beech Rd. DT3: Upwey 6E 19
Beechwood La. DT1: Pound 5E 11
Beechwood Sq. *DT1: Pound ...5F 11*
(off Beechwood La.)
Beel Cl. DT5: Fort 1E 31
Belfield Cl. DT4: Weym 5E 27
Belfield Pk. Av. DT4: Weym ...6E 27
Belfield Pk. Dr. DT4: Weym ...6E 27
Belgrave DT4: S'hill 6E 23
Belgrave Pl. DT5: Fort 2E 31
Bellever Ct. DT1: Pound 4F 11
Belle Vue DT4: Weym 4H 27
Belle Vue Ct. *DT4: Weym 5G 27*
(off Belle Vue Rd.)
Belle Vue Rd. BH19: Swan 5H 41
DT4: Weym 6G 27
Belle Vue Ter. DT5: Fort 3E 31
Bell's Orchard La.
BH20: Ware 5E 37
Bell St. BH19: Swan 4E 41
Belmont St. DT4: Weym 5H 27
Belvedere Rd. BH19: Swan ...5H 41
Benlease Way BH19: Swan ...4D 40
Ben Nevis Rd. DT4: Weym 5F 27
Benville Rd. DT4: Weym 4C 26
Bere Rd. BH20: Ware 4D 36
Berkeley Ct. DT6: Bridp 5C 4
Berrylands DT2: Cross 3C 34
Besent Wlk. DT2: Cross 2C 34
BESTWALL 6F 37
Bestwall Cres. BH20: Ware 6F 37
Bestwall Rd. BH20: Ware 6F 37
Beverley Rd. DT3: Lit 1G 23
Biddlecome Orchard
DT6: Bridp 3B 4
Big Ope DT5: Fort 2D 30
Billingsmoor La.
DT1: Pound 5F 11
Bilshay La. DT6: Dot 1A 4
Bincleaves Ct. *DT4: Weym 5G 27*
(off Bincleaves Rd.)
Bincleaves Rd. DT4: Weym ...5G 27
BINCOMBE 4A 20
Bincombe Ct. DT3: Lit 2H 23
Bincombe Ri. DT3: Lit 1H 23
Bindells, The DT3: Chick 1A 26
Bindon La. BH20: Wool 5H 35
Bindon Way BH20: Wool 5H 35
Binghams Rd. DT2: Cross 2C 34
Birch Way DT2: Charl D 2G 9
DT3: Over 4B 24
Birchwood Tourist Pk.
BH20: Cold H 1A 36
Birley Hall BH19: Swan 1H 41
Bishops Cl. DT3: A'bury 3G 7
Bishop's Rd. DT3: A'bury 3H 7
Bishops Row BH19: Swan 4F 41
Blackberry La. DT3: Broadw ...1F 23
Blacknor Rd. DT5: Westo 1D 32
Blagdon Cl. DT2: Mart 2A 14
Blagdon Rd. DT1: Dor 5G 11
Blenheim Rd. DT3: Red 3E 23
Blind La. DT3: A'bury 2G 7
Blind La. Cl. DT6: Bradp 1E 5
Blindmere Rd. DT5: Westo ...6D 30
Blockhouse La. *DT4: Weym ...3H 27*
(off New St.)
Bloomfield Ter. DT5: E'ton 6F 31
Bockhampton La.
DT2: Higher B, Lwr B,
Stin, W Staf 4H 13
DT2: W Staf 4H 13
Bodkin La. DT3: Over 4B 24
Bohay's Dr. DT4: Wyke 1D 28
Boleyn Cres. DT4: Weym 1F 29
Bolton Pl. DT6: Bridp 5C 4
Bon Accord Rd.
BH19: Swan 5G 41
Bond St. DT4: Weym 3G 27
(not continuous)
Boney Rd. BH20: Bovin 1E 35
Bonfields Av. BH19: Swan 2G 41
Bonnett's La. BH20: Ware 5E 37
Bonscombe La. DT6: Ship G ...6H 5
Boscawen Cen. DT5: Cas 1E 31
Bothen Dr. DT6: Both 5D 4
BOTHENHAMPTON 1C 6
Bothenhampton Nature Reserve
....................2D 6
Boulton Cl. DT4: Wyke 6E 27
Boundary Cl. BH19: Swan 6H 41
Bourne Dr. BH20: Ware 3D 36
BOVINGTON 1F 35
BOVINGTON CAMP 1E 35
Bovington La. BH20: Bovin ...2E 35
Bow, The DT1: Dor 4B 12
Bowers Rd. DT5: Westo 1D 32
Bowhayes DT6: Both 6D 4
BOWLEAZE 3D 24
Bowleaze Coveway
DT3: Over 4C 24
Bowling All. Wlk. DT1: Dor ...5B 12
Bown Hill DT5: S'well 3D 32
Brackendown Av. DT3: Over ...4A 24
BRADFORD PEVERELL 6C 8
Bradford Rd. DT4: Weym 4E 27
BRADPOLE 2F 5
Braemar Rd. DT1: Dor 6D 12
Bramble Dr. DT6: Bridp 3C 6
Bramble Drove
DT2: Broadm 6H 17
Bramble Edge DT2: Broadm ...6H 17
Brambling Cl. DT3: Broadw ...6F 19
Bramley Hill DT6: Bridp 3D 4
Brandy La. DT5: Fort 3D 30
Brandy Row DT5: Fort 3D 30
Branscombe Cl. DT5: S'well ...2D 32
BRAYTOWN 6F 35
Breaches La. BH20: Corfe C ...1G 39
Breach Fld. BH20: Wool 5G 35
Breston Cl. DT5: S'well 3D 32
Brewer's Quay *4H 27*
(off Hope Sq.)
Brewer Wlk. DT2: Cross 2C 34
Brian Cl. BH20: Sand 1G 37
Briar Cl. DT4: S'hill 1D 26
Briars End DT2: Cross 2D 34
Brickyard La. BH19: Swan 1F 41
Bridge Ct. DT1: Dor 4C 12
Bridge Inn La. DT3: Pres 1D 24
Bridlebank Way
DT3: Broadw 1E 23
BRIDPORT 5C 4
Bridport Arts Cen. 5C 4
BRIDPORT COMMUNITY HOSPITAL
.......................3A 4
Bridport Leisure Cen. 6B 4
Bridport Mus. 5C 4
Bridport Rd.
DT1: Dor, Pound 5E 11
DT2: Dor 5A 10
Brisbane Rd. DT3: Lit 2H 23
Briston Cl. DT1: Pound 5F 11
Britannia Way DT1: Dor 6H 11
Brit Vw. Rd. DT6: W Bay 3A 6
Brixey's La. BH20: Ware 5E 37
Broadcroft Gdns.
DT5: E'ton 6G 31
Broadlands Rd.
DT3: Broadw 2E 23
Broad La. DT6: Lwr E, Watt 6A 4
BROADMAYNE 5G 21
Broadmead DT2: Broadm 5G 21
Broadmead Av. DT6: Bridp 4B 4
Broadmeadow Rd.
DT4: Wyke 1E 29
Broad Rd. BH19: Swan 4H 41
BROADWEY 1E 23
Broadwey Cl. DT3: Broadw 6F 19
Broken Cross DT2: Charm 6H 9
Brook Cl. DT2: Charm 5G 9
Brookhouse St. DT1: Pound ...5G 11
Brooklands Farm Conservation Cen.
.......................1E 9
Brookmead Cl. DT3: Sut P 6E 21
Brookside Cl. DT3: Pres 2D 24
Brookton La. DT3: Lit 1G 23
Broomhill Drove
DT2: Broadm 2F 21
Broughton Cres. DT4: Wyke ...1D 28
Brownlow St. DT4: Weym 2G 27
Brown's Cres. DT3: Chick 1B 26
Brunel Ct. DT1: Dor 5B 12
Brunel Dr. DT3: Pres 1C 24
Brunswick Ter. DT4: Weym ...2H 27
Brutus Cl. DT1: Dor 1H 15
Bryants La. DT4: Wyke 6D 26
Brydian Ct. *DT6: Bridp 4C 4*
(off Barrack St.)
Brymers Av. DT5: Fort 3E 31
Bryn Rd. BH20: Sand 1G 37
DT4: Weym 4E 27
Buckbury M. DT1: Dor 6C 12
Buckingham Way DT1: Dor ...6D 12
BUCKLAND RIPERS 2B 22
Buddleia Cl. DT3: Lit 2A 24
Budmouth Av. DT3: Over 4B 24
Budmouth Community Sports Cen.
......................3B 26
Bull Cl. DT2: Strat 4B 8
Bumpers La. DT5: E'ton 6G 31
Burlington Rd. BH19: Swan ...2H 41
Burnham's La. BH20: Knit 1C 40
Burnside DT2: Mart 2A 14
Burns Rd. BH20: Ware 3D 36
Burn Vw. DT2: Charm 1A 12
Burraton Sq. DT1: Pound 5G 11
Burraton Yd. *DT1: Pound 5G 11*
(off Burraton Sq.)
Burr Stone Mead
BH19: Swan 4G 41
(off High St.)
BURTON 2A 12
Burton Cl. BH20: Wool 5F 35
Burton Cross Rdbt.
BH20: Wool 6E 35
Burton Rd. BH20: Wool 6E 35
DT1: Dor 3A 12
DT6: Both, Burt B 1C 6
Burton Wood BH20: Wool 6F 35
Burt's Pl. BH19: Swan 4H 41
Bushey La. BH20: Corfe C 1E 39
Bush Rd. DT2: Dor 1F 15
Butchers Cl. DT2: K'ton M 3F 13
Buttercup Way DT6: Bridp 3C 6
Buxton Cl. DT4: Weym 6E 27

Buxton Rd.—Crossways Ct.

Buxton Rd.
DT4: Weym, Wyke 6E 27

C

Caernarvon Cl. DT1: Dor 6D 12
Caesar Grn. DT1: Dor 1H 15
Calcraft Rd. BH20: Corfe C 3B 38
Caledonian Cl. DT4: Weym 1G 27
Caley Way DT6: Bradp 2F 5
Cambridge Ct. DT4: Weym 2B 26
Cambridge Rd. DT1: Dor 5G 11
DT4: Weym 2B 26
Cambridge Wlk.
DT1: Pound 5G 11
Camden Way DT1: Dor 1H 15
Came Down Cl.
DT3: Broadw 1F 23
Came Vw. Cl. DT1: Dor 6E 13
Came Vw. Rd. DT1: Dor 6E 13
Campion Cl. DT4: Weym 6H 23
Camp Rd. DT4: Wyke 1B 28
Canberra Cres. DT3: Lit 1H 23
Canberra Rd. DT3: Lit 2H 23
Canteen Rd. DT5: Cas 1G 31
Canterbury Cl. DT4: Weym 3C 26
Capitol Cl. DT1: Dor 6H 11
Capper Rd. E. BH20: Bovin 1E 35
Capper Rd. W. BH20: Bovin 1E 35
Capston Fld. BH19: Lang M 4A 40
Carey App. BH20: Ware 4D 36
Carey Cl. BH20: Ware 4D 36
Carey Rd. BH20: Ware 3A 36
Carisbrooke DT4: S'hill 1E 27
Carlton Rd. Nth. DT4: Weym 1G 27
Carlton Rd. Sth. DT4: Weym 1G 27
Caroline Pl. DT4: Weym 3G 27
Carpenters Cl. DT2: Strat 4B 8
Carriages, The *DT4: Weym 2H 27*
(off Victoria St.)
Carrick Cl. DT1: Dor 6D 12
Carrington Cl. DT4: Weym 6E 27
Carrion La. BH20: Ware 5E 37
Caseberry Ct. *DT1: Pound 5G 11*
(off Longmoor St.)
Cassea Ct. DT3: Upwey 5F 19
Cassiobury Rd. DT4: Weym 2G 27
Casterbridge Cl.
BH19: Swan 4D 40
Casterbridge Ind. Est.
DT1: Dor 4C 12
Casterbridge Rd. DT1: Dor 6E 13
Castle Cl. DT1: Dor 5G 11
Castle Cove Caravans
DT4: Weym 1G 29
Castle Cove Sailing Club 1F 29
Castlehill Rd. DT4: Wyke 6D 26
Castlemaine Rd. DT3: Lit 2H 23
CASTLE PARK 1H 15
Castle Rd. DT5: Cas, Fort 2D 30
Castle Sq. DT6: Bridp 6B 4
CASTLETOWN 1E 31
Castletown DT5: Cas 1E 31
Caswell Ct. DT3: Lit 2A 24
Caters Pl. DT1: Dor 4B 12
Cauldon Av. BH19: Swan 2G 41
Cauldron Barn Cvn. Pk.
BH19: Swan 2F 41
Cauldron Barn Rd.
BH19: Swan 2G 41
Cauldron Cres. BH19: Swan 2G 41
Cauldron Mdws.
BH19: Swan 2G 41
Causeway DT4: S'hill 4D 22
Causeway Cl. BH20: Ware 4D 36
DT4: S'hill 5D 22
Cecil Rd. BH19: Swan 4F 41
Cedar Cl. BH20: Wool 5G 35
Cedar Dr. BH20: Sand 1G 37
DT3: Pres 2C 24
DT5: S'well 3E 33
Cedar Rd. DT1: Dor 4H 11
DT2: Charl D 2G 9
Celandine Cl. DT4: Weym 6G 23
Celtic Cres. DT1: Dor 1H 15
Cerne Villa Mobile Home Pk.
DT3: Chick 2A 26
Chafeys Av. DT4: S'hill 1D 26
Chafeys Rdbt. DT4: S'hill 1E 27
Chaffinch Cl. DT3: Broadw 1G 23
Chalbury Cl. DT3: Over 2B 24
Chalbury Lodge DT3: Pres 2C 24
Chalk Pit La. BH20: Wool 6F 35
Chalky Rd. DT2: Broadm 2F 21
Challacombe Sq.
DT1: Pound 4F 11
(off Challacombe St.)
Challacombe St.
DT1: Pound 4E 11
Chamberlaine Rd.
DT4: Wyke 6D 26
Chancery La. DT6: Bridp 5C 4
Chandler Cl. DT3: Rad 4G 23
Channel Vw. Rd. DT5: E'ton 6E 31
Channons Ct. DT1: Dor 4B 12
Chapel Cl. DT2: Broadm 5G 21
Chapelhay Hgts.
DT4: Weym 4G 27
Chapelhay Steps
DT4: Weym 4G 27
(off North Quay)
Chapelhay St. DT4: Weym 4G 27
Chapel La. BH19: Swan 4G 41
DT3: A'bury 3G 7
DT3: Osm 1H 25
DT3: Upwey 5F 19
Chardsmead Ct. *DT6: Bridp 4C 4*
(off North St.)
Chards Mead Rd.
DT6: Bridp 4B 4
Charles St. DT1: Dor 4B 12
DT4: Weym 2G 27
CHARLESTOWN 3B 26
Charlmont Cross
DT2: Broadm 5H 21
Charlotte Cl. DT2: Charm 1H 11
CHARLTON DOWN 2G 9
CHARMINSTER 6H 9
Charmouth Pl. DT5: E'ton 5H 31
Chartwell DT4: S'hill 6E 23
Chaseborough Sq.
DT1: Pound 5G 11
Chelmsford St. DT4: Weym 2G 27
Chelwood Ga. DT4: Weym 3B 26
Cherrybrook La.
DT1: Pound 5E 11
Cherry Cl. BH20: Sand 1H 37
Cherry Tree DT6: Bridp 3A 4
Cherry Tree La. DT6: Bridp 2A 4
Cherry Way DT3: Over 4B 24
Chesil Beach Cen. 4E 29
Chesil Beach Holiday Village
DT4: Wyke 3D 28
Chesil Beach Rdbt.
DT4: Wyke 3D 28
Chesil Ho. DT6: W Bay 4B 6
Chesil Pl. *DT1: Dor 5B 12*
(off Somerleigh Rd.)
Chesil Vw. DT4: Wyke 1D 28
Chester Cl. DT1: Dor 6D 12
Chesterfield Pl.
DT3: Upwey 4E 19
DT4: Weym 3H 27
(off The Esplanade)
Chestnut Cl. BH20: Sand 1H 37
Chestnut Pl. DT3: Rad 5F 23
Chestnut Rd. DT2: Charl D 2G 9
DT6: Both 1C 6
Chestnut Way DT1: Dor 4G 11
Cheyne Cl. DT5: S'well 3D 32
CHICKERELL 6A 22
Chickerell Rd. DT3: Chick 1A 26
DT4: Weym 4D 26
Chilbury Gdns. DT2: Ower 6A 34
CHISWELL 2D 30
Chiswell DT5: Fort 2D 30
Christ Church Ct. DT1: Dor 4A 12
Christmas Cl. BH20: Ware 6D 36
Church Acre DT1: Dor 4C 12
Church Cl. BH19: Swan 4G 41
DT1: Dor 4B 12
(off Church St.)
DT2: Brad P 6C 8
DT6: Bradp 2E 5
Church Grn. BH20: Ware 6E 37
Church Hill BH19: Swan 4G 41
Churchill Cl. DT4: Wyke 6D 26
Church Knap DT4: Wyke 6D 26
Church La. BH20: Ware 6E 37
BH20: Wool 5H 35
DT2: Charm 6G 9
DT2: Ower 6A 34
DT2: Stin 3F 13
DT3: Buck R 2A 22
DT3: Osm 1H 25
DT5: S'well 3E 33
Church Ope Rd. DT5: E'ton 1G 33
Church Pas. *DT4: Weym 4G 27*
(off St Edmund St.)
Church Rd. DT3: Pres 1E 25
Church St. BH20: Ware 6E 37
DT1: Dor 4B 12
DT3: A'bury 3G 7
DT3: Upwey 3C 18
DT6: Bridp 5C 4
Church Vw. DT2: Strat 4A 8
Churchward Av. DT3: Pres 1C 24
Cineworld
Weymouth 4G 27
Clare Av. DT3: Chick 4C 26
Claremont Gdns. DT6: Bridp 3C 4
Claremont Rd. DT6: Bridp 3C 4
Clarence Cl. DT5: E'ton 6E 31
Clarence Rd. DT1: Dor 6A 12
DT4: Weym 5C 26
DT5: E'ton 6E 31
Clarendon Av. DT3: Red 3F 23
Claudius Cl. DT1: Dor 1H 15
Clayton Cl. DT3: Lit 1G 23
Cleal's Bldgs. *DT6: Bridp 6C 4*
(off South Wlk.)
Clearmount Rd. DT4: Weym 6F 27
Clements La. DT5: Fort 2D 30
Cleveland Av.
DT3: Rad, Weym 5G 23
DT4: Weym 5G 23
Cleverlawns DT3: A'bury 3E 7
Cleves Cl. DT4: Weym 1F 29
Cliff Av. BH19: Swan 1H 41
Cliff Pl. BH19: Swan 4H 41
Cliff Way DT5: S'well 3C 32
Clifton Cl. BH19: Swan 2H 41
Clifton Pl. DT4: Weym 3G 27
Clifton Rd. BH19: Swan 2G 41
Clive Ter. DT4: Weym 3E 27
Clivia Cl. DT3: Lit 2H 23
Clovens Rd. DT5: Fort 3E 31
Cluny Cres. BH19: Swan 4H 41
Clyffe Vw. DT2: Cross 2C 34
Coastguard Cotts. DT5: Fort 2D 30
Coastguard Rd. DT5: Fort 2D 30
Cobham Dr. DT4: Weym 2C 26
Cobblers La. BH19: Swan 5G 41
Coburg Ct. DT1: Dor 6A 12
Coburg Pl. DT4: Weym 3G 27
Coburg Rd. DT1: Dor 5G 11
Cocklands DT2: Charm 6H 9
Cockles La. DT4: Wyke 6B 26
(not continuous)
COKER'S FROME 3C 12
Colchester Way DT4: Weym 3C 26
COLD HARBOUR 1A 36
COLDHARBOUR 5B 22
College Cl. DT3: Binc 4A 20
College La. DT4: Weym 1H 27
Collett Cl. DT3: Pres 1C 24
Colletts Cl. BH20: Corfe C 4B 38
Collier's La. BH20: Wool 6F 35
Collins La. DT4: Wyke 1D 28
Colliton Pk. *DT1: Dor 4A 12*
(off The Grove)
Colliton St. DT1: Dor 4B 12
Colliton Wlk. DT1: Dor 4A 12
Cologne Rd. BH20: Bovin 1F 35
Colwell Shop. Cen.
DT4: Weym 3G 27
Combe Way DT2: Cross 3C 34
Comet Cl. DT4: Weym 5C 26
Commercial Rd.
BH19: Swan 4H 41
DT4: Weym 2G 27
Compass Ter. DT5: S'well 4D 32
Compton Ct. DT3: Rad 6G 23
Concorde Cl. DT4: Weym 5C 26
CONEYGAR 3C 4
Coneygar Cl. DT6: Bridp 3C 4
Coneygar La. DT6: Bridp 3
Coneygar Pk. DT6: Bridp 4
Coneygar Rd. DT6: Bridp 3
Conifers, The DT1: Dor 4H
Conifer Way DT4: S'hill 6D
Coniston Cres. DT3: Rad 5
Connaught Gdns.
DT4: Weym 5E
Connaught Rd. DT4: Weym 5
Conniger La. BH20: Ware 6
Conway Dr. DT2: Broadm 5G
Conway Wlk. DT1: Dor 6D
COOMBE 4E
Coombe Av. DT4: Weym 6G
Coombe Hill BH19: Lang M 4E
Coombe La. DT6: Loders 3
Coombe Valley Rd.
DT3: Pres 6E
Coombe Way DT2: Cross 2C
Cooper's Cl. BH20: Ware 5E
Coopers Ct. *DT6: Bridp 4*
(off Nth. Alling
Coopers Dr. DT6: Both 2
Coppice, The DT3: Chick 6E
Coppice Ct. DT3: Broadw 1
Corbin Way DT6: Bradp 1
Cordova Gdns. DT6: Bridp 4
CORFE CASTLE 3E
Corfe Castle 2A
Corfe Castle Model Village &
Gardens 2A
Corfe Castle Mus. 2B
Corfe Castle Station
Swanage Railway 2B
Corfe Rd. DT3: Red 4E
Cornflower Cl. DT3: Lit 2A
Cornhill DT1: Dor 4E
Cornhill Way DT3: Sut P 6D
Cornwall Cl. DT4: Weym 3D
Cornwall Rd. BH19: Swan 4H
DT1: Dor 4A
Coronation Cres. DT3: Rad 5F
Coronation Rd. DT3: Rad 5F
DT5: Fort 2E
DT6: Bridp 6
Corporation Rd. DT4: Weym 3E
Corscombe Cl. DT4: Weym 3G
Corvesgate BH19: Swan 1G
Cottage Cl. BH20: Wool 5G
Courtauld Dr. DT4: Weym 6E
Court Barton DT5: Westo 6D
Court Cl. DT6: Bradp 2
Courtenay Cl. BH20: Ware 3F
Courtlands Rd. DT5: Westo 1D
COURT ORCHARD 3
Court Orchard Rd. DT6: Bridp 3
Court Rd. BH19: Swan 4F
DT3: Broadw 2E
Courtyard, The DT5: S'well 3C
Cove Cotts. DT5: Fort 3D
Cove Pas. DT4: Weym 4H
Cove Row DT4: Weym 4H
Cove St. DT4: Weym 4H
Coward's La. DT3: A'bury 3
Cow La. BH19: Swan 4F
BH20: Ware 6E
Cowlease BH19: Swan 4F
Cowleaze DT2: Mart 2A
Cowleaze Rd. DT2: Broadm 6G
Cowley Cl. DT1: Dor 5H
Crack La. BH19: Lang M 3B
Cranborne Rd. BH19: Swan 3G
Cranford Av. DT4: Weym 6H
Cranford Ho. DT4: Weym 1H
Creech Way DT3: Red 4E
Crescent St. DT4: Weym 2H
Crewkerne Pl. *DT6: Bridp 5*
(off Chancery
Crispins Cl. DT4: Wyke 6D
Crock La. DT6: Both 6
Croft, The BH20: Ware 6F
Croft Rd. DT5: Westo 6D
Cromwell Rd. DT1: Dor 6B
DT4: Weym 3F
Cross, The BH20: Wool 5H
Cross Rd. DT4: Weym 5F
Crosstree Cl. DT2: Broadm 6G
CROSSWAYS 3C
Crossways Ct. DT2: Cross 3C

44 A-Z Weymouth

Frome Ter. DT1: Dor 4B **12**
Frome Valley Rd.
DT2: Cross 2B **34**
Frome Vw. DT2: Brad P 6D **8**
FROME WHITFIELD 2B 12
Frome Whitfield Cotts.
DT2: Frome W 2A **12**
Fulbrooks Cl. DT6: Bridp 4B **4**
Fulbrooks La. DT6: Bridp 4B **4**
Furbers Paddock DT2: Strat 4B **8**
Furlands DT5: E'ton 1E **33**
Furzy Cl. DT3: Over 3C **24**

G

Gables, The DT1: Dor 4A **12**
Gabriel Cotts. DT2: W Kni 3H **21**
Gabriel Grn. DT1: Dor 6C **12**
Gale Cres. DT6: Bridp 6B **4**
Gallows Hill DT2: Ower 6A **34**
Gallwey Rd. DT4: Wyke 1D **28**
Gannetts Pk. BH19: Swan 3G **41**
Garden Cl. DT6: Bridp 4C **4**
Garfield Av. DT1: Dor 6H **11**
Garfield La. BH19: Lang M 4A **40**
Garibaldi Row *DT4: Weym 4F **27***
(off Weston Rd.)
Garland Cres. DT1: Dor 6C **12**
Garlands Ct. *DT1: Dor 4B **12***
(off Princes St.)
Garnet Ct. *DT4: Weym 3G **27***
(off Park St.)
Garston Hill DT3: Chick 6A **22**
Garwoods BH19: Swan 2G **41**
Gascoyne La.
DT2: Brad P, Wrac 1D **10**
Gatcombe Cl. DT1: Dor 6D **12**
Geelong Cl. DT3: Lit 2H **23**
Gemma Ct. DT4: Weym 3E **27**
George St. DT6: W Bay 3B **6**
Georgian Cl. DT3: Broadw 6E **19**
GIDDY GREEN 5E 35
Giddy Grn. La. BH20: Wool 5E **35**
Giddy Grn. Rd. BH20: Wool 5E **35**
Gilbert Ct. BH19: Swan 4G **41**
Gilbert Rd. BH19: Swan 4G **41**
Giles Cl. DT2: Brad P 6D **8**
Giles Cross DT2: Brad P 1E **11**
Gipsy La. DT6: Bridp 2D **4**
Glacis DT5: Fort 3F **31**
Gladiator Grn. DT1: Dor 1H **15**
Gladstone Cl. DT3: Lit 2H **23**
DT6: Bridp 4D **4**
Glebe Cl. DT3: A'bury 3H **7**
DT3: Osm 2H **25**
DT4: Weym 5F **27**
DT6: Both 6C **4**
Glebefields DT2: Brad P 5C **8**
Glebeford Cl. DT2: Ower 6B **34**
Glebeland Cl. DT2: W Staf 6H **13**
Glebe Way DT2: W Kni 4H **21**
Glen Av. DT4: Weym 4F **27**
Glendinning Av.
DT4: Weym 1G **27**
Glenmore Rd. DT4: Weym 2E **27**
Glennie Way DT3: Chick 2A **26**
Globe Cl. BH19: Swan 4E **41**
Globe La. DT6: Bridp 5C **4**
Gloucester Cl. DT4: Weym 3B **26**
Gloucester M. DT4: Weym 3G **27**
Gloucester Rd. DT1: Dor 5H **11**
Gloucester Row *DT4: Weym 3G **27***
(off Gloucester M.)
Gloucester St. DT4: Weym 3G **27**
Glyde Ct. *DT1: Dor 4B **12***
(off Glyde Path Rd.)
Glyde Path Rd. DT1: Dor 4B **12**
Goldcrest Cl. DT3: Broadw 6F **19**
Goldcroft Av. DT4: Weym 2F **27**
Goldcroft Rd. DT4: Weym 1E **27**
Gordon Cres. DT4: Weym 4C **26**
Gordon Rd. BH19: Swan 4F **41**
Gordon Row DT4: Weym 4G **27**
Gore Cross Bus. Pk.
DT6: Bradp 1D **4**
Gore Cross Way DT6: Bradp 2E **5**
Gore Hill BH20: Sand 1F **37**
Gore La. DT6: Bradp 1E **5**
Gore Ter. DT6: Bradp 1F **5**
Goss Pl. DT4: Weym 2F **27**
Gould's Hill DT2: Dor 5C **14**
DT3: Upwey 2D **18**
Goulds Hill Cl. DT3: Upwey 3D **18**
Governors La. DT4: Weym 4H **27**
Grafton Av. DT4: S'hill 6D **22**
Granby Cl. DT4: Weym 3C **26**
Granby Ct. DT4: Weym 2C **26**
Granby Ind. Est.
DT4: Weym 2B **26**
(not continuous)
Granby Way DT4: Weym 1D **26**
Grangecroft Rd.
DT5: Westo 1D **32**
Grange Rd. DT4: Weym 1H **27**
Granville Rd. DT4: Weym 4F **27**
Grasmere Cl. DT3: Rad 5E **23**
Grasmere Rd. DT3: Rad 6F **23**
Grays DT4: S'hill 6E **23**
Gt. Cranford St. DT1: Pound 4E **11**
Gt. George St. DT4: Weym 3G **27**
Gt. Ovens Dr. BH20: Ware 3D **36**
Gt. Western Ct. DT1: Dor 5A **12**
Gt. Western Ind. Est.
DT1: Dor 5A **12**
Gt. Western Rd. DT1: Dor 5B **12**
Gt. Western Ter.
DT4: Weym 6G **23**
Grebe Cl. DT3: Chick 1A **26**
Green, The DT2: Strat 4A **8**
Greenacre DT2: Charm 6H **9**
Green Cl. DT6: Bradp 3E **5**
Greenhill DT4: Weym 2H **27**
Greenhill Ct. DT4: Weym 6H **23**
Greenhill Ter. DT5: Fort 2E **31**
Greenings Ct. DT1: Dor 4B **12**
Green La. DT2: Cross 2C **34**
DT3: Chick 1B **26**
DT4: Weym 6F **27**
DT6: Both 6D **4**
DT6: Wald 4F **5**
Greenway Cl. DT3: Red 4F **23**
Greenway Rd. DT3: Red 3F **23**
Greenways DT5: E'ton 1E **33**
Greenwood Ho. DT2: Charl D 2G **9**
Gresham Ct. DT6: Bridp 4B **4**
Greville Ct. DT2: Charl D 2H **9**
Grey School Pas. DT1: Dor 4B **12**
Greystones Cl. DT2: Cross 2C **34**
Grosvenor Cres. DT1: Dor 6B **12**
Grosvenor Rd. BH19: Swan 5H **41**
DT1: Dor 6B **12**
DT4: Weym 1G **27**
DT5: E'ton 6E **31**
GROVE 5H 31
Grove, The DT1: Dor 3A **12**
DT3: Broadw 1E **23**
DT5: E'ton 5H **31**
Grove Av. DT4: Weym 6G **23**
Grove Ct. DT1: Dor 3A **12**
Grove Flds. DT5: E'ton 5G **31**
Grove La. DT3: A'bury 4G **7**
DT6: Wald 5G **5**
Grove Point DT5: E'ton 5H **31**
Grove Rd. DT5: E'ton 5F **31**
Grove Ter. DT4: Weym 3E **27**
Grove Trad. Est. DT1: Dor 3A **12**
Guernsey St. DT5: Fort 3E **31**
Gully BH19: Swan 4C **40**
Gundry La. DT6: Bridp 5B **4**
Gundry Rd. DT6: Both 4E **5**
Gypshayes BH19: Lang M 4A **40**
Gypsy La. DT4: Weym 4F **27**
DT5: Westo 1E **33**

H

Haley Ct. DT4: Weym 4E **27**
Halstock Cl. DT3: Pres 2D **24**
Halves Cotts.
BH20: Corfe C 4B **38**
Hambro Rd. DT5: Fort 3E **31**
Hambro Ter. DT3: Pres 1D **24**
Hamcroft DT5: E'ton 6E **31**
Hamilton Cl. DT3: Lit 2H **23**
Hammond Av. DT4: S'hill 6D **22**
Hampshire Rd. DT4: Weym 2C **26**
Hanbury Rd. BH19: Swan 4F **41**
Handborough Cvn. Pk.
DT4: Weym 3B **26**
Hands La. DT3: A'bury 3G **7**
Hannah's La. DT3: A'bury 3F **7**
Hanover Ct. *DT6: Both 5D **4***
(off Lwr. Walditch La.)
Hanover Rd. DT4: Weym 1G **27**
Happy Island Way DT6: Bridp 4E **5**
Harbour Hill DT3: Chick 4C **22**
Harbour Life Mus. 3B 6
Harbour Vw. Rd. DT5: Fort 2E **31**
Hardwick St. DT4: Weym 2G **27**
Hardy Av. *DT1: Dor 4C **12***
(off Kings Rd.)
DT1: Dor 4C **12**
(River Cres.)
DT4: Weym 4E **27**
Hardy Cl. DT2: Mart 2A **14**
Hardye Arc. *DT1: Dor 4B **12***
(off South St.)
DT1: Dor 5B **12**
(Charles St.)
Hardy Rd. BH20: Ware 6D **36**
DT6: Bridp 4D **4**
Hardy's Cottage 1H 13
Hardy's Row DT2: W Kni 3H **21**
Harewood Rd. DT1: Pound 5F **11**
HARMAN'S CROSS 5F 39
Harman's Cross Roads
BH20: Har C 6F **39**
Harman's Cross Station
Swanage Railway 6F 39
Hartlebury Ter. *DT4: Weym 4G **27***
(off Franchise St.)
Harveys Ter. *DT1: Dor 4C **12***
(off Holloway Rd.)
Hascombe Ct. *DT1: Dor 5B **12***
(off Somerleigh Rd.)
Haven, The BH19: Swan 4H **41**
Haven Ct. BH19: Swan 1G **41**
Hawkesworth Cl. DT3: Pres 1C **24**
Hawthorn Cl. DT1: Dor 4A **12**
DT4: S'hill 6D **22**
Hawthorn Flats DT1: Dor 4H **11**
Hawthorn Rd. DT1: Dor 4H **11**
DT2: Charl D 2G **9**
Haycrafts La. BH19: Har C 6F **39**
Haylands DT5: E'ton 1E **33**
Haylands Cl. DT1: Pound 5F **11**
Haymoor Cl. DT3: Over 4A **24**
Hayward's Av. DT3: Rad 5G **23**
Hazeldown Av. DT3: Over 4A **24**
Hazel Dr. DT3: Pres 2C **24**
Headland Cl. DT5: S'well 3D **32**
Headland Warren
DT1: Pound 4F **11**
Heathcote Cl. DT1: Dor 5C **12**
Heather Cl. BH19: Swan 4F **41**
Heathland Cl. DT2: Cross 3C **34**
Heathwood Rd. DT4: Weym 2E **27**
Helen La. DT4: Weym 4H **27**
Hemlet's Cl. DT6: Bradp 2E **5**
Henchard Ct. DT1: Dor 4A **12**
Henchard Ho. DT1: Dor 4H **11**
Hendrie Cl. BH19: Swan 3E **41**
Henry Cl. DT4: Weym 6F **27**
Herbert Pl. DT4: Weym 4G **27**
Hereford Cres. DT4: Weym 3D **26**
Hereford Rd. DT4: Weym 3D **26**
Hermitage Ct. DT1: Pound 5F **11**
Heron Cl. DT3: Chick 1A **26**
DT3: Over 4C **24**
Heron Ct. DT4: Weym 2G **27**
DT6: W Bay 4B **6**
Herringston Barn
DT2: Win H 5A **16**
Herringston Rd. DT1: Dor 2A **16**
DT2: Dor, Win H 2A **16**
Herrison Ho. DT2: Charl D 2G **9**
Herrison Rd. DT2: Charl D 3G **9**
HERSTON 4E 41
Herston Cvn. & Camp Site
BH19: Swan 2E **41**
Herston Cross BH19: Swan 3E **41**
Herston Halt Station
Swanage Railway 3E 41
Herston Yards Farm Camping Site
BH19: Swan 2D **40**
Hessary Pl. DT1: Pound 5
Hessary St. DT1: Pound 5
Hetherly Rd. DT3: Rad 5
Hexworthy Ct. DT1: Pound 4
Hibbs Cl. BH20: Ware 4
Hibernia Cl. DT6: Bridp 3
Highacres DT6: Loders 2
Highcliffe Rd. BH19: Swan 2H
Highdown DT3: Over 4A
Highdown Av. DT1: Pound 5G
High East St. DT1: Dor 4E
HIGHER BOCKHAMPTON 1H
Higher Day's Rd.
BH19: Swan 4D
Higher End DT3: Chick 1A
Higher Filbank
BH20: Corfe C 4E
Higher Gdns. BH20: Corfe C 3E
Higher La. DT5: Fort 2D
Higher St. DT6: Bradp 2
Higher Wood BH20: Bovin 1E
Highfield Cl. DT2: Charm 5
Highgrove Cl. DT1: Dor 6C
Highland Rd. DT4: Weym 3
HIGHLANDS 1
Highlands End Farm Holiday Pk.
DT6: Lwr E 2
High St. BH19: Lang M 4A
BH19: Swan 4C
BH20: Wool 5H
DT1: Dor 4C
DT4: Wyke 6D
DT5: Fort 3E
DT5: S'well 4E
High St. Cl. BH20: Wool 5G
High Trees DT2: Broadm 6H
High W. St. DT1: Dor 4A
DT4: Weym 4G
Hillbourne Cl. DT4: Wyke 1E
Hillbourne Rd. DT4: Wyke 1E
Hill Cl. DT6: W Bay 3
Hillcrest BH19: Swan 5H
Hillcrest Rd. DT4: Weym 1F
Hillfield Cl. DT3: Upwey 6E
Hillfort Cl. DT1: Dor 1H
Hillfort M. *DT1: Dor 1H*
(off Hillfort
Hillingdon DT6: Bridp 3
Hill La. DT4: Weym 4H
Hill Ri. DT6: W Bay 3
Hill Rd. BH19: Swan 1G
Hillsea Rd. BH19: Swan 4F
Hillside Rd. BH20: Wool 6F
Hillside Ter. DT1: Dor 5C
Hill Vw. DT2: Charm 6
DT3: Osm 2H
DT6: Bradp 2
Hillview Est. DT6: Bridp 3
Hill Vw. Rd. BH19: Swan 4
Hillyard Ct. *BH20: Ware 6E*
(off Mill
Hintock St. DT1: Pound 5G
Hoburne Pk. BH19: Swan 5F
Hoburne Rd. BH19: Swan 4F
Holbaek Cl. DT1: Dor 1C
Holcombe Cl. DT3: Pres 2E
Holland Rd. DT4: Weym 3F
Hollands Cl. BH20: Corfe C 3A
Hollands Ho. DT1: Dor 4A
Hollands Mead Av.
DT2: Ower 6A
Holloway Rd. DT1: Dor 4C
Hollow Hill
DT2: Higher B, Stin 3F
Hollow Way DT6: Both 1
Holly Cl. BH20: Sand 1G
DT1: Dor 4G
Holly Ct. DT3: Rad 6G
Holly Rd. DT4: Weym 3F
Holmead Wlk. DT1: Pound 5G
Holme Cl. DT3: Red 4E
Holmes Rd. BH19: Swan 4D
Holyrood Ter. DT4: Weym 3F
Honeysuckle Cl. DT3: Lit 2A
Hope Cl. DT2: Cross 3C
Hope Sq. DT4: Weym 4H
Hope St. DT4: Weym 4H
Hope St. Sth. DT4: Weym 4H
Hope Ter. DT2: Mart 2A

Rutland Rd.—Strodes La.

Rutland Rd. DT4: Weym 2E 27
Ryan Bus. Pk. BH20: Ware 4E 37
Ryan Cl. BH20: Ware 4E 37
Ryemead La. DT4: Wyke 2D 28
Ryland's La. DT4: Weym 6E 27
Rymbury DT3: Pres 1D 24

S

St Alban St. DT4: Weym 4G 27
St Aldhelms Ct.
BH19: Swan 3G 41
St Andrew's Av. DT3: Rad 5G 23
St Andrews Church (remains of) 1G 33
St Andrews Cl. DT1: Dor 6C 12
St Andrew's Gdns.
DT6: Bradp 3E 5
(off Shoe La.)
St Andrew's Ind. Est.
DT6: Bridp 3E 5
St Andrew's Rd.
DT6: Bradp, Bridp 4C 4
St Andrew's Ter. DT6: Bradp 3E 5
ST ANDREW'S WELL 3E 5
St Andrew's Well DT6: Bradp 3E 5
St Anne's Rd. DT4: Weym 1F 29
St Catherine's Chapel 4F 7
St Cecilia's Gdns. DT6: Bridp 3C 4
St Davids Cl. DT1: Dor 6C 12
St David's Rd. DT4: Weym 1E 29
St Edmund St. DT4: Weym 4G 27
St Edward's Cl.
BH20: Corfe C 3B 38
St George's Av. DT4: Weym 6H 23
St Georges Cl.
BH19: Lang M 4A 40
DT1: Dor 5E 13
St George's Est. Rd.
DT5: E'ton 6E 31
St Georges Rd. DT1: Dor 5D 12
DT5: E'ton 6E 31
St Georges School Ct.
DT1: Dor 4C 12
(off High St.)
St Helen's Rd. BH20: Sand 1G 37
DT1: Dor 4A 12
DT4: Weym 4C 26
St Helier Av. DT3: Broadw 6E 19
St James Pk. DT6: Bradp 2F 5
St John's Cl. DT5: Fort 3E 31
St John's Ct. *DT4: Weym 2H 27*
(off William St.)
St John's Hill BH20: Ware 6E 37
St Julien Cres.
DT3: Broadw 1E 23
St Katherine's Av. DT6: Bridp 4D 4
St Katherine's Dr. DT6: Bridp 3D 4
St Lawrence Rd.
DT3: Upwey 5F 19
St Leonard's Rd.
DT4: Weym 5G 27
St Luke's Ct. DT6: Bridp 3A 4
St Martins Cl. BH20: Ware 5E 37
DT2: Broadm 5G 21
St Martins Fld. DT2: Mart 1A 14
St Martin's Ho. *BH20: Ware 5E 37*
(off North St.)
St Martin's La. BH20: Ware 5E 37
St Martin's Pl. BH20: Sand 1G 37
St Martin's Rd. BH20: Sand 1G 37
DT4: Weym 6F 27
DT5: Fort 3E 31
St Mary's Cl. BH20: Ware 4C 36
St Mary's Pl. DT6: Bridp 5C 4
St Mary St. DT4: Weym 4G 27
St Michael's Ct. DT4: Weym 5F 27
St Michael's La. DT6: Bridp 5B 4
St Michael's Rd.
BH20: Ware 6E 37
St Michael's Trad. Est.
DT6: Bridp 5B 4
St Nicholas St. DT4: Weym 4G 27
St Osmund's Community Sports Cen. 6C 12
St Patricks Av. DT4: Weym 5C 26
St Pauls Ct. DT4: Weym 3F 27
St Paul's Rd. DT5: Fort 3E 31
St Swithins Av. DT6: Bridp 4B 4
St Swithins Ct. DT6: Bridp 4B 4
St Swithins Rd. DT6: Bridp 4B 4
St Thomas Rd. DT1: Dor 4A 12
St Thomas St. DT4: Weym 4G 27
St Vasts Rd. BH19: Swan 5H 41
Salisbury M. *DT1: Dor 4C 12*
(off High St.)
Salisbury Rd. BH19: Swan 5H 41
DT4: Weym 3F 27
Salisbury St. DT1: Dor 4C 12
Salisbury Ter. *DT1: Dor 4C 12*
(off Salisbury St.)
Salisbury Vs. *DT1: Dor 4C 12*
(off Salisbury St.)
Salisbury Wlk. DT1: Dor 4C 12
Samphire Cl. DT4: Weym 6G 23
Sandbourne Cl. BH19: Swan 4E 41
Sandbourne Rd. DT3: Over 3C 24
Sanderling Cl. DT3: Broadw 6F 19
SANDFORD 1G 37
Sandford La. BH20: Ware 4E 37
Sandford La. Ind. Est.
BH20: Ware 3E 37
Sandford Rd.
BH20: Sand, Ware 4E 37
Sandford Ter. BH20: Sand 1F 37
SANDFORD WOODS 1F 37
Sandhills Cres. BH20: Wool 5E 35
Sandholes Cl. DT5: S'well 3D 32
Sandpiper Way DT4: Wyke 2E 29
Sandringham Ct.
BH19: Swan 4G 41
DT1: Dor 6D 12
Sandringham Sports Cen. 5C 12
Sandsfoot Castle (remains of) 1G 29
Sandsfoot Holiday Pk.
DT4: Weym 6F 27
Sandy Hill La.
BH20: Corfe C, Woolg 2B 38
Sandyholme Holiday Pk.
DT2: Ower 6C 34
Sawmills La. DT1: Dor 1A 16
Sawyers La. DT2: Strat 4B 8
Saxon Ct. BH20: Ware 4E 37
School Cl. DT1: Dor 4B 12
DT3: Chick 6A 22
School Dr. DT2: Cross 2C 34
School Hill DT3: Chick 6A 22
School La. DT1: Dor 4A 12
School St. DT4: Weym 3G 27
Scotton Way, The
DT2: Cross 3C 34
Seamoor Cl. DT3: Over 4A 24
Sea Rd. Nth. DT6: Bridp 5D 4
Sea Rd. Nth. Ind. Est.
DT6: Bridp 4D 4
Sea Rd. Sth. DT6: Bridp 1C 6
Sea Vw. DT5: Fort 2E 31
Seaview Holiday Pk.
DT3: Pres 2E 25
Seaward Gdns. DT6: Bridp 3C 6
Seaward Rd. BH19: Swan 2G 41
Seaway La. DT3: A'bury 3F 7
Second Cliff Wlk. DT6: W Bay 3A 6
Sedgefield Cl. DT4: Weym 3F 27
Sefton Ct. BH19: Swan 4G 41
Selle Rd. BH20: Bovin 1F 35
Selwyn Cl. DT3: Lit 1G 23
Sentry Fld. BH19: Swan 5H 41
Sentry Rd. BH19: Swan 4H 41
Serrells Mead
BH19: Lang M 4B 40
Seven Acres DT5: S'well 3D 32
Seven Acres Rd. DT3: Pres 1D 24
Seven Barrows Rd.
BH20: Ware 3D 36
Seymer Rd. BH19: Swan 4H 41
Seymour Pl. DT6: Bridp 5C 4
Shapley Ct. DT1: Pound 5E 11
Sharpitts DT5: Westo 6D 30
Shaston Cl. BH19: Swan 4E 41
Shaston Cres. DT1: Dor 1C 16
Shatter's Hill BH20: Ware 5E 37
Shaw Dr. BH20: Sand 1F 37
Shears Rd. DT4: Weym 5G 23
Sheepdown Rd. DT1: Pound 4F 11
Shepherds Cft. DT5: E'ton 5H 31
Shepherds Cft. Rd.
DT5: E'ton 5G 31
Sherberton St. DT1: Pound 5E 11
Sherford Cl. BH20: Ware 3D 36
Sherford Dr. BH20: Ware 3E 37
Sherlock Ct. *DT4: Weym 3F 27*
(off Southview Rd.)
Sherren Av. DT2: Charl D 2G 9
SHIPTON GORGE 6H 5
Shipton Rd. DT6: Ship G 5H 5
Shirecroft Rd. DT4: Weym 3D 26
Shirley Cl. BH19: Swan 4E 41
Shirley Ct. DT1: Dor 5H 11
Shirley Rd. BH20: Ware 6D 36
Shoe La. DT6: Bradp 3E 5
Shore Rd. BH19: Swan 3H 41
(not continuous)
Shortlake La. DT3: Osm 3H 25
Shortlands DT5: E'ton 6E 31
Shortlands Rd. DT3: Upwey 5F 19
Short Rd. DT4: Weym 3E 27
Shottsford Cl. BH19: Swan 4D 40
Shrubery La. DT4: Wyke 6D 26
Silent Woman Pk.
BH20: Cold H 1A 36
Silklake M. DT5: E'ton 6F 31
Silver St. DT3: Sut P 6E 21
Simene Cl. DT6: Bridp 4A 4
SKILLING 6B 4
Skilling Hill Rd. DT6: Bridp 6A 4
Skilling La. DT6: Bridp 6A 4
Slades Grn. DT6: Both 6D 4
Slyer's La. DT2: Cok F 3D 12
Smallmouth Cl. DT4: Wyke 3E 29
Smishops La. DT6: Loders 2H 5
Smokey Hole La. DT1: Dor 6D 12
(not continuous)
Sodern La. DT2: Wrac 5E 9
Solent Rd. BH19: Swan 6H 41
Somerleigh Rd. DT1: Dor 4B 12
Somerset Rd. DT4: Weym 2D 26
Sorrel Cl. DT4: Weym 6H 23
Souter Way DT3: Rad 4G 23
South C'way. BH20: Stob 6E 37
Southcliffe Rd.
BH19: Swan 6H 41
South Ct. Av. DT1: Dor 6B 12
Southcroft Rd. DT4: Weym 5C 26
Southdown Av. DT3: Over 4A 24
Southdown Est. DT3: Over 4A 24
Southdown Rd. DT4: Weym 6F 27
South Drove DT2: Broadm 1H 21
(not continuous)
Southfield Av. DT4: Weym 6G 23
Southfield Ho. DT1: Dor 5B 12
SOUTHILL 6D 22
Southill Garden Dr.
DT4: S'hill 6E 23
Sth. Instow BH19: Har C 6G 39
SOUTHLANDS 6F 27
Southlands Rd. DT4: Weym 6F 27
Sth. Lawns DT6: Both 6C 4
South M. *DT6: Bridp 5C 4*
(off Church St.)
Sth. Mill La. DT6: Bridp 6C 4
South Pde. DT4: Weym 4H 27
South Pk. DT4: Weym 2B 26
South Rd. BH19: Swan 4F 41
DT4: Wyke 2D 28
South St. BH20: Ware 6E 37
DT1: Dor 5B 12
(not continuous)
DT6: Bridp 5C 4
South Ter. DT1: Dor 5B 12
South Vw. DT2: Broadm 5H 21
Southview Rd. DT4: Weym 3E 27
South Wlk. DT6: Bridp 6B 4
South Walks DT1: Dor 5B 12
Sth. Walks Rd. DT1: Dor 5B 12
South Way DT5: S'well 3C 32
SOUTHWELL 3D 32
Southwell DT5: S'well 3E 33
Southwell Bus. Pk.
DT5: S'well 3C 32
Southwell Rd. DT5: S'well 3F 33
Spa Av. DT3: Rad 5F 23
Spadger La. *DT2: W Staf 6H 13*
(off Barton M.)
Sparacre Gdns. DT6: Bridp 4C 4
Spa Rd. DT3: Rad 5
DT4: Rad 5
Spiller Rd. DT3: Chick 1
Spinnaker Vw. DT4: Weym 4
Spinners' La. DT6: Wald
Spinney, The DT2: Broadm 6
DT3: Broadw 2
Spitfire Cl. DT2: Cross 3
Spring Av. DT4: Weym 5
Springbrook Cl.
BH20: Har C 6
Spring Cl. DT6: Bradp
Springfield Cres.
DT3: Broadw 1
Springfield M. *BH19: Swan 4*
(off High
Springfield Rd.
BH19: Swan 4
DT3: Broadw 1
Spring Gdns. DT2: Broadm 4
DT4: Weym 5
DT5: Fort 3
Springham Wlk.
DT1: Pound 5
Springhill *BH19: Swan 4*
(off High
Spring La. DT4: Weym 5
Spring Rd. DT4: Weym 5
Springrove Ct. DT4: Weym 1
Spring St. BH20: Wool 5
Springwell Cl.
BH20: Corfe C 3
Square, The BH19: Swan 4
BH20: Corfe C 2
BH20: Wool 5
DT2: Charm 6
DT2: Strat 4
DT5: S'well 3
Stafford Cl. DT2: W Kni 3
Stafford Gdns. DT2: W Staf 6
Stafford Rd. BH19: Swan 4
Stainforth Cl. DT4: Weym 3
Stalls, The DT3: Chick 6
Standfast Wlk. DT1: Dor 6
Stanier Rd. DT3: Pres 1
Stanley Pl. *DT6: Bridp*
(off King
Stanley St. DT4: Weym 2
Stanton Ct. DT4: Weym 1
Station App. DT1: Dor 5
Station Pl. BH19: Swan 4
Station Rd. BH19: Swan 4
BH20: Wool 5
DT5: E'ton 6
DT6: W Bay
Stavordale Bus. Pk.
DT4: Weym 3
Stavordale Ct. DT4: Weym 3
Stavordale Rd. DT4: Weym 3
Steeple Cl. DT3: Red 4
Steepways BH19: Swan 5
Steer Rd. BH19: Swan 4
Steppes BH19: Lang M 3
Steppes Hill BH19: Lang M 4
Stevensons Ct. DT6: Bridp
STINSFORD 3
Stinsford Cotts. DT2: Stin 3
Stinsford Hill DT2: Stin 4
Stinsford Vw. DT1: Dor 5
Stirling Rd. DT3: Red 4
Stoborough Cl. DT3: Red 4
Stockley Rd. BH20: Ware 3
Stokehouse St. DT1: Pound 5
Stoke Rd. DT4: Wyke 1
Stonechat Cl. DT3: Broadw 6
Stonehill Ct. DT4: Wyke 1
Stone Ho. *DT1: Dor 4*
(off Pound
Stottingway St. DT3: Upwey 5
Stour Dr. BH20: Ware 3
Stowcastle St. DT1: Pound 5
Stowell Cres. BH20: Ware 6
Stowey St. DT1: Pound 5
Straits DT5: E'ton 6
Strand, The DT6: Bridp 5
STRATTON 4
Streche Rd. BH19: Swan 1
BH20: Ware 6
Strodes La. DT2: Charl D 2

50 A-Z Weymouth

Column 1

udley Cres. DT3: Pres 1D 24
art Way DT6: Bridp 4E 5
dland Rd. BH20: Corfe C ..1B 38
dland Way DT3: Red 4E 23
ton Rd. DT4: Weym 6F 27
cliffe Ct. BH19: Swan ...2H 41
dew Cl. DT4: Weym 6H 23
ningdale Ri. DT3: Over ...3C 24
nybank DT6: Bridp 4B 4
nydale Rd. BH19: Swan ..6H 41
nyfields DT3: Sut P 6D 20
nyside Rd. DT4: Wyke 1D 28
ridge Cl. DT4: Weym 4G 41
shine Wlk. BH19: Swan ..4G 41
rey Cl. DT4: Weym 2C 26
ssex Rd. DT4: Weym 2E 27
cliffe Av. DT4: S'hill 6D 22
til Cres. DT6: Pym 1D 4
ton Cl. DT3: Sut P 6D 20
ton Ct. Lawns
   DT3: Sut P 6D 20
ton Rd. DT3: Pres 1E 25
TON POYNTZ 6E 21
ton Rd. DT3: Pres 1E 25
affield Gdns. DT4: Wyke ..6D 26
ains Row DT6: W Bay 3B 6
allow Cl. BH20: Wool 5F 35
allow Ct. DT4: Weym 3F 27
ANAGE 4G 41
anage Bay Vw. Holiday Pk.
   BH19: Swan 5F 41
anage Coastal Pk.
   BH19: Swan 5E 41
ANAGE COMMUNITY HOSPITAL
   ....5G 41
anage Mus. 4H 41
anage Railway
   Corfe Castle Station ...2B 38
   Harman's Cross Station
   ....6F 39
   Herston Halt Station ..3E 41
   Norden Station 1A 38
anage Sailing Club 4H 41
anbridge Ct. DT1: Dor ..4C 12
anbridge Mobile Home Pk.
   DT1: 4B 12
anbrook M. BH19: Swan .4G 41
annery Bri. DT4: Weym ..3G 27
annery Rd. DT6: Bridp ...5B 4
eet Hill La. DT5: S'well ..3D 32
eethill M. DT5: S'well ...5C 4
eet Hill Rd. DT5: S'well ..4D 32
camore Cl. BH20: Sand ..1H 37
camore Rd. DT4: S'hill ...6D 22
denham Cres.
   BH20: Wool 5F 35
denham Rd. BH19: Swan ..4D 40
denham Way DT1: Dor ...5C 12
dney St. DT4: Weym 3E 27
monds Cl. DT3: Rad 5G 23
monds Ct. DT2: Charm ...6H 9
ward Cl. DT1: Dor 5E 13
ward Rd. DT1: Dor 6D 12

T

bit's Hill La.
   BH20: Har C, Woolg 6F 39
bothays Rd. DT1: Dor ...6C 12
botts DT2: Broadm 5G 21
lidge Cl. DT3: Pres 1E 25
mlin St. BH20: Sand 1G 37
nk Mus. 2E 35
nners La. BH20: Ware 6F 37
nnery Rd. DT6: Bridp 5B 4
ntinoby La. BH20: Ware ..3D 36
nyard, The DT6: Bridp 5C 4
rrant Dr. BH20: Ware 3D 36
nton Rd. BH19: Swan ...4H 41
witon Ct. DT1: Pound 5F 11
wny Cl. DT3: Broadw 1G 23
wrr Av. DT3: Chick 1A 26
can Way DT4: Weym 3C 26
ddy Bear Mus. 4B 12
   (off Antelope Wlk.)
eling Rd. DT3: Rad 5G 23
tford Cl. DT3: Pres 2C 24
mple Cl. DT1: Dor 6A 12

Column 2

Tennyson Rd. DT4: Weym 4F 27
Terminus Rd. DT4: Weym ...2G 27
Terrace, The DT2: Mart 1A 14
Terracotta Warrior's Mus. 4C 12
   (off High E. St.)
Thatch Cotts. DT3: Osm 2H 25
The ....
   Names prefixed with 'The' for
   example 'The Alisons' are
   indexed under the main name
   such as 'Alisons, The'
Third Cliff Wlk. DT6: W Bay ...3A 6
Thomas Hardye Leisure Cen.
   ....6G 11
Thomas Hardy Quarters
   BH20: Bovin 1F 35
Thomson Cl. DT6: Bridp 4A 4
Thorncombe Wood Nature Reserve
   ....1H 13
Thornhill Cl. DT1: Dor 1H 15
Thornhill Cres. DT4: Weym ..2F 27
Thornlow Cl. DT4: Weym ...6E 27
Thrasher's La.
   BH20: Corfe C 1C 38
Thread Mill La. DT6: Pym ...1D 4
Three Acre La.
   BH19: Lang M 4C 40
Three Yards Cl. DT5: Fort ..3E 31
Tilbury Mead BH20: Corfe C ..4B 38
Tillycombe Rd. DT5: Fort ...3F 31
Tilly Whim La. DT2: Brad P ..5B 10
Timewalk 4H 27
   (off Hope Sq.)
Tinker's La. BH20: Ware 5E 37
Tinten La. DT1: Pound 5F 11
Tithe Barn Children's Farm, The
   ....4G 7
Toby's Cl. DT5: E'ton 1E 33
Tollerdown Rd. DT4: Weym ..4C 26
Toms Fld. Camping Site
   BH19: Lang M 5A 40
Toms Fld. Rd.
   BH19: Lang M 4A 40
Toms Mead DT2: Corfe C ..3A 38
Tourist Info. Cen.
   Bridport 5C 4
   Dorchester 4B 12
   Purbeck 6E 37
   Weymouth 3H 27
Tout Hill BH20: Bovin, Wool ..3G 35
Tout Quarry Sculpture Pk. ...4E 31
Town Hall La. BH19: Swan ..4G 41
Town La. DT3: A'bury 3E 7
TOWN'S END 4B 38
Townsend Mead
   BH20: Corfe C 4B 38
Townsend Nature Reserve ..5F 41
Townsend Rd. BH19: Swan ..4G 41
   BH20: Corfe C 4B 38
Townsend Way DT6: Bradp ..1E 5
Tradecroft DT5: Westo 5E 31
Tradecroft Ind. Est.
   DT5: Westo 5D 30
Trenchard Way DT3: Chick ..1A 26
Trent Dr. BH20: Ware 3D 36
Treve Mnr. Units DT1: Dor ..4B 12
   (off Somerleigh Rd.)
Treves Rd. DT1: Dor 6H 11
TRIMAR HOSPICE 6E 37
   (off Pound La.)
Trinity Cl. BH20: Ware 6E 37
   (off Trinity Ter.)
Trinity Ct. DT4: Weym 4G 27
Trinity La. BH20: Ware 6E 37
Trinity St. DT1: Dor 4B 12
   DT4: Weym 4H 27
Trinity Ter. DT4: Weym 4G 27
Trinity Way DT6: Bradp 2E 5
Trocadero BH19: Swan 4H 41
   (off High St.)
Trustin Cl. DT6: Bridp 3A 4
Tudor Arc. DT1: Dor 4B 12
Tunis Ter. DT6: Bradp 2E 5
Turnstone Cl. DT3: Broadw ..6G 19
Turton St. DT4: Weym 3G 27
Tutankhamun Exhibition ...4B 12
   (off High W. St.)
Twelveman's Way DT1: Dor ..6C 12

U

Ullswater Cres. DT3: Rad 5E 23
ULWELL 1F 41
Ulwell Cott. Cvn. Pk.
   BH19: Swan 1E 41
Ulwell Rd. BH19: Swan 1G 41
Underbarn Wlk. DT4: Weym ..6G 27
Underhedge Gdns.
   DT5: S'well 3D 32
Union Ct. DT4: Weym 4F 27
Uplands DT6: Wald 5F 5
Up. Fairfield Rd. DT2: Corfe ..5B 12
Upway St. DT4: Weym 2G 27
UPWEY 5E 19
Upwey Station (Rail) 1F 23

V

Valley Cl. DT3: Pres 1E 25
Valley Rd.
   BH19: Har C, Lang M ...5C 38
   BH20: Corfe C, Har C ..5C 38
   DT6: Both 1C 6
Vanguard Av. DT4: Weym ..5C 26
Vearse Cl. DT6: Bridp 6A 4
Ventnor Rd. DT5: Fort 2E 31
Verlands Rd. DT3: Pres 1E 25
Verne, The DT5: Fort 2F 31
Verne Cl. DT4: Weym 5F 27
Verne Comn. Rd. DT5: Fort ..3E 31
Verne Hill Rd. DT5: Fort ...3E 31
Verne Rd. DT4: Weym 5F 27
Verne Way DT4: Weym 5F 27
Vernons Ct. DT6: Bridp 6B 4
   (off Normandy Way)
Vespasian Way DT1: Dor ...1H 15
Vicarage Cl. BH20: Wool ...6G 35
Vicarage Ct. DT6: Bridp ...3B 4
Vicarage Gdns. DT2: Charm ..6H 9
Vicarage La. DT1: Dor 4C 12
   (off Holloway Rd.)
   DT2: Charm 6H 9
Victoria Av. BH19: Swan ...3E 41
   DT3: Upwey 5E 19
Victoria Av. Ind. Est.
   BH19: Swan 3E 41
Victoria Bldgs. DT1: Dor ...4C 12
   DT5: Fort 2D 30
Victoria Ct. DT1: Dor 5A 12
Victoria Flats DT1: Dor 5A 12
   (off Dagmar Rd.)
Victoria Gro. DT6: Bridp ...4B 4
Victoria Pl. DT5: E'ton 5F 31
Victoria Rd. BH19: Swan ...1H 41
   DT1: Dor 5A 12
   DT4: Wyke 1D 28
   DT5: E'ton 5G 31
Victoria Sq. DT5: Fort 2D 30
Victoria St. DT4: Weym 2H 27
Victoria Ter. BH19: Swan ...4E 41
   DT1: Dor 4C 12
   DT4: Weym 2H 27
   (off Victoria St.)
Victor Jackson Av.
   DT1: Pound 5F 11
Victory Ct. DT1: Dor 4B 12
   (off North Sq.)
Victory Rd. DT5: Fort 2D 30
Village Rd. DT6: Bradp 2E 5
Village St. DT3: Osm 1H 25
Vindelis Ct. DT5: Fort 2E 31
Vines Pl. DT4: Weym 4C 26
Viscount Rd. DT4: Weym ...5C 26
Vivian Pk. BH19: Swan 2G 41
Vulcan Cl. DT4: Weym 5C 26

W

Waddon Way DT6: Loders ...1H 5
Wainwright Cl. DT3: Pres ..1C 24
Wakeham DT5: E'ton 6F 31

Column 4

WALDITCH 5F 5
Walditch Rd.
   DT6: Both, Wald 5D 4
Walker Cres. DT4: Wyke ...2D 28
Wallsend Cl. DT5: S'well ...2D 32
Walls Vw. Rd. BH20: Ware ..4D 36
Walpole St. DT4: Weym ...2G 27
Walrond Rd. BH19: Swan ..3G 41
Wanchard La. DT2: Charm ..5F 9
Wanderwell DT6: Bridp 1C 6
Wanderwell Farm La.
   DT6: Both 1C 6
Wardbrook St. DT1: Pound ..5G 11
Wardcliffe Rd. DT4: Weym ..3F 27
WAREHAM 6E 37
WAREHAM COMMUNITY HOSPITAL
   ....6D 36
Wareham Rd.
   DT2: Ower, Wareh 6A 34
Wareham Station (Rail) 4D 36
Wareham Town Mus. 6E 37
Warmwell Cvn. Pk.
   DT2: Warm 4C 34
Warmwell Leisure Resort
   DT2: Warm 4B 34
Warmwell Rd. DT2: Cross ..3C 34
Warmwell Ski Slope 4A 34
Warne Hill DT6: Bridp 4E 5
Warren Cl. DT4: Weym 4C 26
Washpond La. BH19: Swan ..3D 40
Watergates La.
   DT2: Broadm 5H 21
Waterloo Pl. DT4: Weym ...2H 27
   (off Victoria St.)
Water Mdw. La. BH20: Wool ..4E 35
WATERMEADOWS 4D 12
Waterside Holiday Pk.
   DT3: Over 3D 24
Watery La.
   DT3: Broadw, Upwey ..6E 19
   DT5: Westo 1E 33
Watford La.
   DT6: Bradp, Pym 1D 4
WATTON 1A 6
Watton Gdns. DT6: Bridp ..3D 4
Watton La. DT6: Watt 1A 6
Watton Pk. DT6: Bridp 6B 4
Watton Vw. DT6: Bridp 4A 4
Waverley Ct. DT3: Rad 6G 23
Waverley Rd. DT3: Rad 6F 23
Weare Cl. DT5: Fort 3E 31
Weatherbury Way DT1: Dor ..1B 16
Webbers Cl. BH20: Corfe C ..3A 38
Wedgwood Rd. DT4: Weym ..3F 27
Weighbridge Ct.
   BH19: Swan 4H 41
Weir, The DT3: Pres 1D 24
Weir End Rd. DT1: Pound ..4F 11
Weir Vw. DT2: Charm 6F 9
Weld Ct. DT1: Dor 5B 12
Welland Ct. DT1: Pound ...5G 11
   (off Middlemarsh St.)
Wellbridge Cl. DT1: Dor ...1B 16
Wellfields Dr. DT6: Bradp ..3E 5
Wellington Cl. DT4: Weym ..4H 27
Wellstead Rd. BH20: Ware ..3D 36
Wentworth Cl. DT3: Lit 2H 23
Wesley St. DT4: Weym 3G 27
Wessex Oval BH20: Ware ...4C 36
Wessex Rd. DT1: Dor 5G 11
   DT4: Weym 3E 27
Wessex Rdbt. DT4: Weym ..2C 26
Wessex Stadium 1C 26
Wessex Way BH19: Swan ...2G 41
   DT1: Dor 4H 11
West Allington DT6: Bridp ..4A 4
WEST BAY 4B 6
W. Bay Cres. DT4: Wyke ...1D 28
W. Bay Holiday Pk.
   DT6: W Bay 3A 6
W. Bay Rd.
   DT6: Bridp, W Bay ...6C 4
Westbourne Rd.
   DT4: Weym 1G 27
Westbrook Vw. DT3: Upwey ..5E 19
W. Cliff Est. DT6: W Bay ...3A 6
W. Cliff Rd. DT6: W Bay ...3A 6
Westcliff Rd. DT5: Westo ..1D 32
Westcott St. DT1: Pound ...4E 11

The representation on the maps of a road, track or footpath is no evidence of the existence of a right of way.